Lyrics & Love Songs

Also from Westphalia Press
westphaliapress.org

Lyrics & Love Songs

Gen. Albert Pike and the Old Canoe Controversy

by Albert Pike

with a new introduction by Paul Rich

WESTPHALIA PRESS
An imprint of Policy Studies Organization

Westphalia Press
An imprint of Policy Studies Organization
1527 New Hampshire Ave., NW
Washington, D.C. 20036
info@ipsonet.org

ISBN-13: 978-1941755907
ISBN-10: 1941755909

Cover design by Taillefer Long at Illuminated Stories:
www.illuminatedstories.com

Daniel Gutierrez-Sandoval, Executive Director
PSO and Westphalia Press

Devin Proctor, Director of Media and Publications
PSO and Westphalia Press

Updated material and comments on this edition
can be found at the Westphalia Press website:
www.westphaliapress.org

This New Edition is dedicated to
Charles Kreiner,
an expert on old canoes
as well as many other things.

Introduction
General Albert Pike and
the Old Canoe Controversy

Few Freemasons in the nineteenth century could equal Albert Pike in learning and literary output.[1] Although we most often think of Pike in connection with the Scottish Rite of Freemasonry, of which he was so long the head, it would be a great mistake to think that was the limit of his influence. There could hardly be a better example of an Enlightenment figure than Pike. "That Masonry is in some sense the product of the Enlightenment is beyond dispute. Because Albert Pike was a great Freemason, and a great scholar of the Craft," writes Peter Paul Fuchs, "then we would expect him in some way to be an Enlightenment product." Given Pike's hundreds of books and articles, that referencing of the Enlightenment is easily demonstrated.[2]

Pike was indeed exceptional and stories about him are not only extraordinary but also often true. Typically in his larger than life character, he attended his own funeral wake in Washington in 1859 when a rumor that he was dead caused his grieving friends to organize a farewell banquet. Since all was in place for the wake, news that he was alive did not keep the event from going ahead and Pike appeared dramatically after a number of libations had been consumed. Rather than annoyed, he thought the experience useful: "I am wiser than before, and know men better. I know them better, and therefore love them more, and would fain do the world and my fellows some service before I die."[3]

G

Pike intrigues not only Masons but those outside the Craft. He was not a Puritan. Craig Parshall in the novel *The Rose Conspiracy*, describes Pike's colorful career as a focal point for his own Washington thriller: "A man who bragged of being conversant in numerous languages, well-read in the world religions and philosophies, and an international leader among the Freemasons, Albert Pike met, and was most certainly captivated by, Vinnie Ream, the pretty, coquettish sculptor who had wooed Washington's high society. During their long relationship, Pike arranged for Ream to ceremonially receive Masonic degrees, despite the fact that women were generally forbidden from joining the Masons."[4]

We just possibly could speculate that memories of a long affectionate relationship with Vinnie were why, when asked, Pike attributed the poem *The Old Canoe* to a young lady. Well, it was by a young lady but not by Vinnie Ream. The poem is still attributed here and there to Pike, but when Dallas Herndon of the Arkansas History Commission made a study of the matter, he concluded that it was by Thomas Worthen, who died in Little Rock, Arkansas, when he was only twenty-five. Worthen wrote under the pen name of *Alciphhon*. A Col. J.N. Smithee, editor of the *Arkansas Gazette*, had published the poem and attributed it to Pike, who denied the honor. Herndon followed in the footsteps of Fred W. Allsopp, who in 1933 tried to settle the matter in favor of Worthen in his *The Poets and Poetry of Arkansas*.

In preparing this edition we discovered that the poem was actually by Emily R. Page (1838-1860) of Bradford, Vermont. She wrote it when she was only eighteen. The daughter of a canal toll keeper, she was depicting a real scene near her home. She wrote for a number of Boston periodicals.[5]

H

This collection is the 1916 edition of *Lyrics and Love Songs*, which first appeared as edited by Pike's daughter, Lilian Pike Roome (1843-1919), in 1899 and was copyrighted by her and Allsopp. Allsopp wrote *The Life Story of Albert Pike* in 1920 and *Albert Pike: A Biography* in 1928. The addition of the note by Mrs. Roome makes this volume of considerable bibliographical interest. *The Old Canoe* is a remarkably good poem, and that Pike acknowledged that it was not of his doing is a compliment to his truthfulness. That others still tried to identify him as the author is an indication of the respect held for him.

Paul Rich
Garfield House, Washington

I

NOTES

1 The literature about Pike is voluminous, but a short tour of his genius at ritual is offered in Jim Tresner, Vested in Glory, Scottish Rite Research Society, Washington DC, 2000, with paintings by Robert H. White.

2 Peter Paul Fuch, "Incense to the Intellect: Implications of the Albert Pike Library", Heredom, Vol.17, 2009, 78.

3 Robert Duncan, Reluctant General, Dutton, New York, 1961, 50.

4 Craig Parshall, The Rose Conspiracy, Harvest House, Eugene (Oregon), 2009, 79.

5 Harper's Cyclopaedia of British and American Poetry. Epes Sargent, 1881, 887. See Silas McKeem. A History of Brdaford, Vermont, 1875. Moses Foster Sweetser, The White Mountains, 1886 , 318. Abby Maria Hemenway, Poets & Poetry of Vermont, George A. Tuttle, 1858, 350.

J

LYRICS AND LOVE SONGS

by

GEN. ALBERT PIKE

EDITED BY MRS. LILIAN PIKE ROOME
Daughter of the Author

ILLUSTRATED

———

LITTLE ROCK, ARKANSAS
FRED W. ALLSOPP
1916

GEN. ALBERT PIKE
(From a Photo by Sarony, New York)

CONTENTS
LYRICS AND LOVE SONGS

PREFACE.

Before we issued the first edition of my father's poems, I had commenced collecting material for a complete biography of him; and a part of this material was used by me to write the biographical sketch which served as a preface to the poems. When we concluded to issue the second edition, having considered the matter carefully, I felt that the time had come to complete the full biography, and to edit the prose writings, publishing the entire collection as the Life and Works of General Albert Pike. Mr. Allsopp assured me of his entire accord with these views, and the present edition is the result of our hearty co-operation. I thought it would be a good plan to have the Life and Recollections precede the prose writings, and I hope the public will approve of this innovation. The announcement of the forthcoming edition, with the full life and prose writings, in addition to the complete collection of his poems, was heartily welcomed by the friends and admirers of my father in every section of the country, which has been a great encouragement to me in such an important undertaking. I have been specially careful to "nothing extenuate nor aught set down in malice," and have edited the writings with the utmost care and conscientiousness; and the readers may rely upon the absolute correctness of any statement made by me as of my own knowledge.

LILIAN PIKE ROOME,
Washington, D. C., April 15, 1916.

OFFICE OCCUPIED BY GEN. ALBERT PIKE
As Grand Commander, Southern Division Scottish Rite, Washington, D. C.

EVERY YEAR.

Life is a count of losses,
> Every year;
For the weak are heavier crosses,
> Every year;
Lost Springs with sobs replying
Unto weary Autumns' sighing,
While those we love are dying,
> Every year.

The days have less of gladness,
> Every year;
The nights more weight of sadness,
> Every year;
Fair Springs no longer charm us,
The winds and weather harm us,
The threats of Death alarm us,
> Every year.

There come new cares and sorrows,
> Every year;
Dark days and darker morrows,
> Every year;
The ghosts of dead loves haunt us,
The ghosts of changed friends taunt us,
And disappointments daunt us,
> Every year.

To the Past go more dead faces,
> Every year;
As the loved leave vacant places,
> Every year;

Everywhere the sad eyes meet us,
In the evening's dusk they greet us,
And to come to them entreat us,
            Every year. .

"You are growing old," they tell us,
            "Every year;
"You are more alone," they tell us,
            "Every year;
"You can win no new affection,
"You have only recollection,
"Deeper sorrows and dejection,
            "Every year."

Too true!—Life's shores are shifting,
            Every year;
And we are seaward drifting,
            Every year;
Old places, changing, fret us,
The living more forget us,
There are fewer to regret us,
            Every year.

But the truer life draws nigher,
            Every year;
And its Morning-star climbs higher,
            Every year;
Earth's hold on us grows slighter,
And the heavy burthen lighter,
And the Dawn Immortal brighter,
            Every year.

MONUMENT TO GEN. ALBERT PIKE
Erected by the Scottish Rite Masons in Washington, D. C., 1899

AS THE SEASONS COME AND GO.

The fresh young leaves are coming, Dear!
　In the genial prime of May;
And the bees in the blooms are humming, Dear,
　And the world is glad and gay;
Is gay and glad, in the ripe bright Spring;
　Forgetting the Winter-snow;
But Winter again the snows must bring,
　As the Seasons ebb and flow;
And so the world goes round in a ring,
　As the Seasons come and go.

As the Seasons come and go, and the years
　One after another die,
With wan sad faces wet with tears,
　And the laugh that ends in a sigh;
In a sigh, — and, sighing, our hopes and joys
　Pace after them, sad and slow,
With our manhood's baubles and childhood's toys,
　As the Seasons ebb and flow,
Leaving us only the pleasure that cloys,
　As the Seasons come and go.

The lads are the fair girls wooing, Dear!
  In the rath glad days of Spring,
And the graybeards for young loves suing, Dear!
  While the thrushes, mating, sing.
They are wise, — for the Young grow old and gray,
  And Time is a fair girl's foe;
And maids are fickle, and men will stray,
  As the Seasons ebb and flow;
For Love's Forever is but a day,
  As the Seasons come and go.

In the new Love's lap all the old are forgot,
  When the mouth new kisses craves;
They are gone, like prayers remembered not,
  One after one, like the waves:
On the dead Loves' ashes the live Loves tread,
  And into its fires we throw
The false girl's pictures, the tress of the Dead!
  As the Seasons ebb and flow,
Forgetting the once-sweet lips so red,
  As the Seasons come and go.

No! No!—there *were* Loves we cannot forget,
    Charming faces, forever dear;
Sweet lips, with whose kissing ours tingle yet,
    Loving words we shall always hear;
Eyes that we always shall look into,
    Whether they love us or no;
Adorations immortal, tender and true,
    Though the Seasons ebb and flow;
Immortal, O Darling! as mine for you,
    While the Seasons come and go.

TO A ROBIN.

Written in New Mexico on hearing the song of the only Red-breast I ever saw there.

Hush, where art thou clinging,
And what art thou singing,
Bird of my own native land?
Thy song is as sweet as a fairy's feet
Stepping on silver sand.
And thou art now
As merry as though thou wert singing at home,
Far away, in the spray
Of a warm shower raining through odorous gloom;
Or as if thou wert hid, to the tip of thy wing,
By a broad oaken leaf in its greenness of Spring,
With thy nest lurking 'mid a gray heaven of shade,
To protect thy dear young from all harm fitly made.

Hush, hush! Look around thee!
Bleak mountains impound thee,
Cliffs gloomy, rocks barren and dead;
A desolate pine doth above thee incline,
But yields not a leaf for thy bed,
And lo! below,
No flowers of beauty or radiance bloom,
But weeds, — grayheads, —
That mutter and moan when the wind-tides loom.
And the rain never falls in the warm, sunny Spring,
To freshen thy heart or to strengthen thy wing.
But thou livest a hermit these deserts among,
Where Echo alone makes reply to thy song.

And while thou art chanting,
  With head thus up-slanting,
    Thou seemest a thought or a vision,
That flits with quick haste o'er the heart's lonely waste,
    With an influence soothing, elysian:
      Or a lone sweet tone,
  That sounds for a time in the ear of sorrow; —
      Ah! soon, too soon,
  I must bid thee a long and a sad good morrow: —
But if thou wilt turn to the South thy wing,
I will meet thee again at the end of Spring,
And thy nest may be made where the peach and the vine
Shall shade thee, and tendril and leaf shall entwine.

  Art thou not a stranger, and darer of danger,
    That over these mountains hast flown? —
For the land of the North is the clime of thy birth,
    And here thou, like me, art alone.
      Go back on thy track; —
    It were wiser and better for thee and me,
      Than to moan, alone,
    So far from the waves of our own bright sea; —
Then the eyes that we felt to grow dim, months ago,
Will greet us again with their idolized glow.
Let us haste, then, sweet bird, to revisit our home,
Where the oak-leaves are green, and the sea-waters foam.

1832.

THE DEAD CHILD.

The young leaf lives in Spring its little hour,
    And falleth from the limb—who knoweth why?
The fair young bud blooms not into a flower,
    But sickening droops and hasteneth to die.
                            Who knoweth why?
Our Father knows, from whom the bud and leaf
Received their life, so beautiful and brief.

Those loved by us, — the young, fair, innocent, —
    When like your dear ones they have grown more dear,
For but a little season to us lent,
    He calleth home, letting us live on here—
                            Who knoweth why?
They in the early morning of Life's day
Do fade and fade, while we grow old and gray.

Our Father knows.   He knew they did not need
    Life's discipline and sorrow's chastening pain
To make them fit for Heaven, and early freed
    These pure white souls to Him returned again,
                            For us to intercede.
Thus we, amid Life's sorrows, toils and cares,
Have entertained his angels unawares.

    Washington, March 28, 1884.

MA TRISTE CHÉRIE.

Your wondrous eyes look sadly into mine,
Look anxiously and eagerly in mine, —
Look like a sorrowing angel's into mine,
    Until mine ache and fill with bitter tears.
O, what a tale of sadness and of sorrows,
    Those dear eyes tell, —of days that seem like years,
Of nights of sighs, and of unwelcome morrows,
    Of doubts and pain and griefs and heavy fears!

Your amber eyes look, darkening, into mine,
Fixed and dilating, deeply into mine,
Look questioning, beseeching, into mine,
    Until my heart aches with a heavy pain.
I feel the pangs of your soul's crucifixion,
    And in the echoing chambers of my brain,
The words that told me of your great affliction
    Continually repeat their sad refrain.

Darling! the crown of thorns is yours to wear;
Life is a cross, that you must bravely bear;
A burden of long griefs and constant care,—
    The penalty that Genius always pays.
Lean on my love! let it your burthen lighten!
    When the clouds darken, hope for better days!—
Hath love no radiant influence to brighten,
    For heavy hearts, the dark world's painful ways?

Look not so sadly, Darling, in my eyes!
Look not so mournfully into my eyes!
With piteous entreaty, in my eyes:
 Yet turn not yours away, for in their light
Is all my life, and all my joy of living;
 Is all that make the day not sombre night!—
O eyes so true, so loving and forgiving,
 Laugh once again, and make the dark world bright!

O sad, sweet eyes! O stars that light my soul!
O eyes that saturate with love my soul!
That fill with pain and sympathy my soul!
 Ye hold me like a captive bound in chains.
O sweet, fair face, sweetest when melancholy!
 Sweet lips that tremble with unuttered pains!
O Soul of Innocence, sublime and holy!
 Your sorrows pass, but still the trace remains.

O helpless Love! that cannot help the one!
O fruitless Love! that cannot bless the one,
That cannot comfort or console the one,
 Who is the idol of its adoration!
Why should there be no healing in caresses,
 No power to comfort in my life's oblation,
When one kind word from you my tired heart blesses,
 One look of love gives me much consolation!

1869.

CHRISTMAS.

The Christmas time is drawing near, the pleasant Christ-
mas time;
Let us hail its coming cheerfully, with a song of rude old
rhyme:
A good rough song, like those that when old England yet
was young,
Under old Saxon rafters with a jolly chorus rung;
And round shall pass the merry glass, grim care we'll drive
away,
And music and the dance shall greet the gladsome Christ-
mas day.

Old feuds we'll bury fathoms deep, old friendships we'll
renew,
And closer cling to those we love, as the ivy to the yew;
There may be Winter out of doors, the keen, cold wind may
sing
Shrilly and sharply, but within the warm heart shall be
Spring;
Kind feelings, like sweet jasmine buds and flowers shall
come again,
And blossom like the summer rose, blessed with a morning
rain.

Had we our way, the good old sports should be revived
once more;
Again should maiden's little feet dance twinkling on the
floor;

While overhead again should hang the dark-green mistleto,
And all lips that strayed under it the forfeit pay, we know.
The Yule-log should again be brought by many a stout,
    strong hand,
And some fair girl should light it, with the last year's sacred
    brand.

Once more should pass the wassail-bowl, of nut-brown ale
    and old,
A sovereign panacea, that, against the winter's cold!
With the nutmeg, toast and ginger:—all the vintage of the
    Rhine
Can neither warm the brain as well nor make dark eyes to
    shine
With half as much mad mischief, or with half as merry
    glee:—
So away with wine! good Yule-tide ale for my sweetheart
    and me!

"And both in town and country, in the cottage and the
    hall,
There should be fires to curb the cold, and meat for great
    and small."
The neighbors should be bidden in, and all have welcome
    true,
And think the good old fashions were far better than the new;
The roasted apples once again should cover all the hearth,
And many a good old-fashioned game make the rafters
    ring with mirth.

And the boar's head dressed with a green silk scarf, and
     with trumpets blown before,
Come marching solemnly along with a carol sung at the
     door;
Then the maidens should the cake cut up, and she who
     found the bean,
Should be, the whole long holidays, a lovely Christmas
     Queen;
With pretty grace and modesty the coronal to wear,
That brings not to the youthful head uneasiness or care.

And the Christmas tree again should grow, and its golden
     fruitage shine,
Around its dark-green glossy leaves; the ivy fondly twine
Its melancholy tendrils round the trunk and every limb,
As sad thoughts cling around the heart, when at night the
     fire burns dim:
Not of holly, bay or laurel—we would have no royal tree—
But the lusty, green Magnolia, fit emblem for the free.

Alas! the good old days are gone! Time blows an adverse
     gale;
On the waves of new strange oceans falls the shadow of
     our sail;
No more old games we play, we crown no fair young Queen
     or King;
'T was a mere idle dream, that through my mind went
     wandering;

Like as the sea-wind softly blows through a shell upon
    the shore,

And makes a low, sweet melody, echo of ocean's roar.

Not all a dream! We can forgive those that have done us
    wrong,

Draw closer to old friends, and make affection's bonds
    more strong;

Create more sunlight on Life's ways, more starlight in the
    heart,

And get us ready for the time when we must hence de-
    part:—

So may we live in peace with all, and when we pass away,

Look back without a bitter thought to this fair Christmas
    Day.

                               1849.

"AFTER THE MIDNIGHT COMETH MORN."

(A song, dedicated to Senorita Carolina Cassard.)

The Years come, and the Years go,
    And the leaves of life keep falling,
        Queridita!
And across the sunless river's flow,
With accents soft and whispers low,
    The friends long lost are calling,
        Queridita!
While Autumn his red glory wears,
And clouds oppress the sky, like cares:—
    But the old griefs die, and new joys are born,
    And always after Midnight cometh Morn.

The Years wake, and the Years sleep,
    And the Past is full of sorrow,
        Queridita!
The thoughtless laughs and the thoughtful weeps,
And each the fruit of his follies reaps,
    For To-day is the Fate of To-morrow,
        Queridita!
But new loves tempt us to forget
The old, and old friends love us yet:—
    So the old griefs die, and new joys are born,
    And always after Midnight cometh Morn.

The Years laugh, and the Years sigh,
　　But the flowers for you are blowing,
　　　　Queridita!
As Girlhood's days go dancing by,
And Womanhood's blithe May is nigh,
　　With hopes and fancies glowing,
　　　　Queridita!
While Love his nets for you prepares,
And lurks to catch you unawares;—
　　And the old griefs die, and new joys are born,
　　And always after Midnight cometh Morn.

The Years live, and the Years die,
　　And all they touch they sadden,
　　　　Queridita!
But still the heart can Time defy,
Hope still with purple flush our sky,
　　And sober friendship gladden,
　　　　Queridita!
And well as we have loved before,
In Autumn we can love once more:—
　　For the old griefs die, and new joys are born,
　　And always after Midnight cometh Morn.
　　　　Querida mia!

　　　　　　　　　　　　1870.

CLEOPÂTRE.

Go! woo the sweet South-wind, vain man!
   The south-wind capricious and gay,
To be steadfast and constant and true,—if you can,—
   To you only, but for a day;
   It will laugh at you, dancing away,
Other lovers to win with caresses;
   Yet as easily keep the gay South-wind you may,
Bringing odors from maidens' soft tresses,
As her, whom so many have loved and adore,
That man's love, for her, has a value no more.

Go! sue for the rose's perfume,
   That no one may share it with you!
And with blushes for you only ask it to bloom,
   When fifty as ardently sue:
   It will laugh with its bright eyes of dew,
Its graceful head coyly inclining,
   As if weary of words that no longer are new,
And to win new adorers designing;
So she hears, whose eyes once her fondness revealed,
And her lips sweet assurance of constancy sealed.

Go! vex, when the red Sunset dies,
  The Evening-Star on her throne,
With your vows of devotion and vain tears and sighs,
  To win her to love you alone!
  Pour your heart out in songs all her own,
And exist only while you behold her!—
  She will smile still, and shine as she always has shone,
Upon all who their folly have told her;
As the eyes that you love so, the bright sweet eyes,
Fain would make, every day, a new heart their prize.

Entreat the brown throstle, in May,
  Staring gravely at you, where he swings
In the tree-top, to sing for you only, to-day,
  The song that to hundreds he sings;
  And the tremulous stir of his wings,
And the gay song say "no" to your suing;
  So your darling less fondly and close to you clings,
So, impatiently, half-hears your wooing;
While for new hearts to win with her soft pleading eyes,
And her sweet ways and words, she unconsciously sighs.

The bee ask, to haunt but one flower;
    The fawn, at but one spring to drink;
Ask the down in the air to be still but one hour,
    The Stars' diamond eyes not to wink!—
    But be not so vain as to think
That the sweet May can long love November;
    The Stars look not back to the brink
Of the blue Sea, lost loves to remember;
The bright-eyed and beautiful waste no regrets
On the Past, which the young heart soon gladly forgets.

Bring back the sweet face: Set it here,
    With the roses a-near, where you write;
That the eyes which have blest you so many a year,
    May never be out of your sight,
    When you work there, by day or by night.
It will change not, though SHE grow disdainful;
    Do not Genius and Beauty to Youth give the right,
To the self-deceived victims though painful,—
To win and to waste a new heart every hour,
Like the breeze and the bird; like the star and the flower.

*TO MARY.

I ken a charming little maid,
    As sweet and winsome as a fairy;
I wadna ask wi' wealth to wed,
    If I could wed wi' thee, Mary!

I've wandered east, I've wandered west,
    As wanton as the winds that vary;
But ne'er was I sae truly blest,
    As when I met wi' thee, Mary!

Like a wee purple violet,
    That hangs its blushing head sae weary,
When wi' sweet dew its leaves are wet,—
    Sae modest, sweet art thou, Mary!

Thy brow is white, as is the mist,
    That sleeps on heaven's forehead starry;
Or mountain snow by sunrise kissed,—
    Thy heart is purer still, Mary!

---

*Said to have been written to the author's future wife when he was courting her.

Thy e'en are like an eagle's e'en,
    That sitteth proudly on his eyrie;
They glitter with a radiant sheen,
    Yet modest as thy heart, Mary!

Upon thy rosy cheek, the soul
    Seems in the gushing tide to vary,
And crimson currents in it roll,
    As though they wad break through, Mary!

If I could press thee in my arms,
    As my wee wife and bonnie fairy
I wadna gi'e for thy sweet charms,
    The warld and a' its wealth, Mary!

How sweetly wad the hours gae by,
    That noo sae solemn are and dreary,
If thou upon my heart didst lie,
    My ain, my loving, dear Mary!

                                    1834.

LIGHTNING.

The breath of the ocean my cradle is,
Which the sun draws up from the blue abyss,
And the upper cold gives it shape and form,
Till it peoples itself with living storm.

And when it has reached the upper air,
I hold its helm while it wanders there;
I lie in the shade of its lifted sail,
And my bark flies swift before the gale.

I coil myself like a quivering snake,
Invisible, on a chaotic lake;
And dwell unseen in the chasms of cloud,
And the vapors that even to earth are bowed.

I frown on the stars with my glittering eye,
And they hide away while the clouds go by;
And while my eye and shape are unseen,
The meteors down to my palace lean.

When my thin cradle is shaken by wind,
And moon and stars lag eyeless behind,
Then do I quiver, and thunders moan,
In their porphyry caves beneath my throne.

I look in the eyes of the winged stars,
And they whirl away in their orbal cars,
And hide afar in the deeps of heaven,
Like water-drops by the tempest driven.

I look on the sun, and he hideth under
The black plumes of my servant Thunder;
And the moon shuts down her silver lid
Over her eye by which tides are fed.

I take the shape of a fiery adder,
And gliding down the swinging ladder
Of cloud, I hiss on the ocean's breast,
And wake it in pain from its azure rest.

I take the form of an arrow of flame,
And pierce the clouds, and make darkness tame;
While the flap of Night's dark, drifting sail
Shakes to the earth the heavy hail.

I dash myself against granite rocks,
And the echoes rush abroad in flocks,
And each with his hoarse and rattling tongue
Hurls back the challenge that Thunder flung.

And often when heaven's cloudless floor
Is as brilliant and bright as the inmost core
Of an angel's snowy soul, I glide
From the lids of the west;—(thus the cheek of a bride

Blushes and burns when *his* step is heard;)—
And still my servant sleeps unstirred,
While the swift Sunset his broad wings shakes
Over horizon-hidden lakes.

And there, all night, I am seen to quiver,
And flash on the surface of Night's broad river,
Out of whose depths I come and go,
While my cradle of cloud is unseen below.

I inspire the earth, the air, the water,
I am parent of life and king of slaughter,
I green the earth, I open the flowers,
I paint them with blushes, and feed them with showers.

I am the heart's ethereal essence,
All life existeth by my presence;
I am the soul of the mighty earth
And give its myriad creatures birth.

I pierce to the heart of the sunken rocks,
And my fire awakens the earthquake shocks;
I am the life of the flowers and buds,
And feed them with air and vapor-floods.

I am eternal, yet change forever;
I wander always, and dissipate never;
Decay and waste no power possess
Over me, the deathless and fatherless.

Unelemental, immaterial,
Less gross than aught that is not ethereal;
And next to spirit in rank am I:
While matter exists I can never die.

1834.

MY NATIVE LAND, MY TENNESSEE.

[WRITTEN FOR MRS. WASHINGTON BARROW.]

The Sunset flings upon the Sea
   Its golden gush of life and light;
The waves with pleasant melody
   On the white sands are sparkling bright;
Old Ocean, round his many isles,
Like a fair infant sleeping smiles;—
   So would I sleep, and dream of thee,
   My own, my native land, my Tennessee!

Tall mountains with their snowy cones,
   Far inland, bathed in sunshine, blaze;
Like gray-haired giants on their thrones,
   Crowned with young dawn's golden rays.
Toward them I lean, and fain would lie
Guarded by those that pierce thy sky,
   Thou dearest land on earth to me,
   My own, my native land, my Tennessee!

Landward and swift the sea-bird flies,
   Dipping his strong and nervous wings
In the blue waves, as home he hies,
   A truant from his wanderings.
He goes to seek his gentle mate,
His young with longing eyes that wait;
   So would I fain haste home to thee,
   My own, my native land, my Tennessee!

Existence!—'tis but toil and strife,—
   Yet I'll not murmur or repine,
So that the Sunset of my life,
   Sweet day! be clear and calm as thine;—
So that I take my last, long rest,
Dear native land, on thy loved breast;
   Land of the gallant and the free!
   My own, my native land, my Tennessee!

1839.

DIXIE.

I.

Southrons, hear your country call you!
Up! lest worse than death befall you!
    To arms! to arms! to arms! in Dixie!
Lo! all the beacon-fires are lighted,
Let all our hearts be now united!
    To arm! to arms! to arms! in Dixie!

        Advance the flag of Dixie!
          Hurrah! hurrah!
    For Dixie's land we'll take our stand,
        To live or die for Dixie!
    To arms! to arms!
        And conquer peace for Dixie!
    To arms! to arms!
        And conquer peace for Dixie!

II.

Hear the Northern thunders mutter!
Northern flags in South winds flutter!
    To arms! to arms! to arms! in Dixie!
Send them back your fierce defiance!
Stamp upon the accursed alliance!
    To arms! to arms! to arms! in Dixie!
        Advance the flag of Dixie! etc.

III.

Fear no danger! shun no labor!
Lift up rifle, pike, and sabre!
    To arms! to arms! to arms! in Dixie!
Shoulder pressing close to shoulder,
Let the odds make each heart bolder!
    To arms! to arms! to arms! in Dixie!
        Advance the flag of Dixie! etc.

IV.

How the South's great heart rejoices
At your cannon's ringing voices;
    To arms! to arms! to arms! in Dixie!
For faith betrayed and pledges broken,
Wrongs inflicted, insults spoken.
    To arms! to arms! to arms! in Dixie!
        Advance the flag of Dixie! etc.

V.

Strong as lions, swift as eagles,
Back to their kennels hunt these beagles!
    To arms! to arms! to arms! in Dixie!
Cut the unequal bonds asunder!
Let them hence each other plunder!
    To arms! to arms! to arms! in Dixie!
        Advance the flag of Dixie! etc.

VI.

Swear upon your Country's altar,
Never to submit or falter;
    To arms! to arms! to arms! in Dixie!
Till the spoilers are defeated,
Till the Lord's work is completed.
    To arms! to arms! to arms! in Dixie!
        Advance the flag of Dixie! etc.

VII.

Halt not till our Federation
Secures among Earth's powers its station!
    To arms! to arms! to arms! in Dixie!
Then at peace, and crowned with glory,
Hear your children tell the story!
      To arms! to arms! to arms! in Dixie!
        Advance the flag of Dixie! etc.

VIII.

If the loved ones weep in sadness,
Victory soon shall bring them gladness;
    To arms! to arms! to arms! in Dixie!
Exultant pride soon banish sorrow,
Smiles chase tears away to-morrow.
    To arms! to arms! to arms! in Dixie!

      Advance the flag of Dixie!
        Hurrah! hurrah!
For Dixie's land we'll take our stand,
      To live or die for Dixie!
To arms! to arms!
      And conquer peace for Dixie!
To arms! to arms!
      And conquer peace for Dixie! ! !

THE MAGNOLIA.

SONG.

What, what is the true Southern Symbol,
  The Symbol of Honor and Right,
The Emblem that suits a brave people
  In arms against number and might?—
'Tis the ever green stately Magnolia,
  Its pearl-flowers pure as the Truth,
Defiant of tempest and lightning,
  Its life a perpetual youth.

French blood stained with glory the Lilies,
  While centuries marched to their grave;
And over bold Scot and gay Irish
  The Thistle and Shamrock yet wave;
Ours, ours be the noble Magnolia,
  That only on Southern soil grows
The Symbol of life everlasting;—
  Dear to us as to England the Rose.

Paint the flower on a field blue as Heaven,
  Let the broad leaves around it be seen,
"SEMPERVIRENS" the eloquent motto,
  Our colors the BLUE, WHITE and GREEN.

Type of Chivalry, loyalty, virtue,
  In Winter and Summer the same,
Full of leaf, full of flower, full of vigor,—
  It befits those who fight for a name.

For a name among Earth's ancient Nations,
  Yet more for the Truth and the Right,
For Freedom, for proud Independence,
  The old strife of Darkness and Light.
Round the World bear the flag of our glory,
  While the nations look on and admire,
And our struggle, immortal in story,
  Shall the free of all ages inspire.

What though many fall in the conflict,
  And our blood redden many a field?
The foe's on our soil, fellow-soldiers!
  And God is our strength and our shield.
Through the fire and the smoke bear our banner
  Ever on, while a fragment remains!
What though we are few and they many?
  THE LORD GOD OF ARMIES STILL REIGNS.

1861.

TO GENEVIEVE.

Of all the rivers of the West,
I love the clear Neosho best;
For there was I first truly blest,
There first in my fond arms I pressed
    My blushing Genevieve.
Her eyes were bright, yet black as night,
And radiant with love's holy light,—
A tender, melancholy pair,
Brilliant as if were throned there
    Twin love-stars of the eve.
How dear to me that rosy mouth,
Sweet as the sweet-brier of the South,—
These little, graceful, dancing feet,
That flew so joyfully to meet
Me, on our old, rude, oaken seat,
    Close to the clear Neosho!

On my fond heart her forehead fair
In trusting fondness pillowed there;
The sunshine, flashing from her hair,
With golden glory filled the air
    That swam round Genevieve.
Her lips divine pressed close to mine,—
Nay, frown not, Dian!—pure as thine
Were soul and heart, and lip and eye;

Pure as an angel of the sky
     Was my sweet Genevieve;—
Her bosom's snowy paradise,
Forbidden to unhallowed eyes,
Beat with devotion on my breast;
And, clasping fondly her slight waist,
Those rosy, loving lips I kissed,
     Chaste as the cold Neosho.

The river murmured in its bed;
The scented clover round us spread;
The birds sang gladly overhead;
Bees at the honeysuckle fed;—
     All loved my Genevieve.
Her petted deer was ever near,
A gentle thing, devoid of fear;
The flowering vines above us made
A silver dusk, half light, half shade,
     From morn till dewy eve.
And there she murmured in my ear
The words I longed and hoped to hear,
Confessing she was all my own,
Which her dear eyes before had shown,
While often we sat there alone,
     Close to the clear Neosho.

Over the lofty Cavanole
The crimson clouds still foam and roll
But she is gone that was the soul,
Illuming like a sun the whole,
    My sweet young Genevieve.
Vanished are those bright hours that rose,
Like golden drifts at day's soft close;
That face no longer greets me here,
Which made these grassy banks so dear,
    I stay behind to grieve.
Yet still I love the tranquil tide,
On which I wooed and won my bride.
Long years have passed since she was there,
Yet I preserve with jealous care,
Our old, rude, twisted oaken chair,
    That hallows the Neosho.

1840.

FAREWELL TO NEW ENGLAND.

Farewell to thee, New England!
  Farewell to thee and thine!
Good-bye to leafy Newbury,
  And Rowley's hills of pine!

Farewell to thee, brave Merrimac!
  Good-bye! old heart of blue!
May I but find, returning,
  That all, like thee, are true!

Farewell to thee, old Ocean!
  Gray father of mad waves!
Whose surge with constant motion
  Against the granite raves.

Farewell to thee, old Ocean!
  I shall see thy face once more,
And watch thy mighty waves again,
  Along my own bright shore.

Farewell the White Hill's summer snow,
  Ascutney's cone of green!
Farewell Monadnock's regal glow,
  Old Holyoke's emerald sheen.

Farewell gray hills, broad lakes, sweet dells,
  Green fields, trout-peopled brooks!
Farewell the old familiar bells!
  Good-bye to home and books!

Good-bye to all! To friend and foe!
  Few foes I leave behind;
I bid to all, before I go,
  A long farewell and kind.

Proud of thee am I, noble land!
  Home of the fair and brave!
Thy motto evermore should stand,
  "Honor, or honor's grave!"

Whether I am on ocean tossed,
  Or hunt where the wild-deer run,
Still shall it be my proudest boast,
  That I'm New England's son.

So a health to thee, New England!
  In a parting cup of wine!
Farewell to leafy Newbury,
  And Rowley's woods of Pine!

1831.

THE WIDOWED HEART.

LACHRYMÆ PONDERA VOCIS HABENT.
TRISTIS ERIS, SI SOLUS ERIS: DOMINÆQUE RELICTÆ
ANTE OCULOS FACIES STABIT, UT IPSA, TUOUS.

Thou art lost to me forever!—I have lost thee, Isadore!
Thy head will never rest upon my loyal bosom more;
Thy tender eyes will never more look fondly into mine,
Nor thine arms around me lovingly and trustingly entwine,—
Thou are lost to me forever, Isadore!

Thou art dead and gone, dear loving wife, thy heart is
still and cold,
And mine, benumbed with wretchedness, is prematurely old;
Of our whole world of love and joy thou wast the only light,
A star, whose setting left behind, ah me! how dark a night!—
Thou are lost to me forever, Isadore!

The vines and flowers we planted, Love, I tend with anxious
care,
And yet they droop and fade away, as though they wanted
air;
They cannot live without thine eyes to feed them with
their light;
Since thy hands ceased to train them, Love, they cannot
grow aright;—
Thou art lost to them forever, Isadore!

Our little ones inquire of me, where is their mother gone,—
What answer can I make to them, except with tears alone!
For if I say, "To Heaven," then the poor things wish to learn
How far it is, and where, and when their mother will return:—
Thou art lost to them forever, Isadore!

Our happy home has now become a lonely, silent place;
Like Heaven without its stars it is, without thy blessed face:
Our little ones are still and sad;—none love them now but I,
Except their mother's spirit, which I feel is always nigh!—
Thou lovest us in Heaven, Isadore!

Their merry laugh is heard no more, they neither run nor play,
But wander round like little ghosts, the long, long Summer-day:
The spider weaves his web across the windows at his will,
The flowers I gathered for thee last are on the mantel still,—
Thou art lost to me forever, Isadore!

Restless I pace our lonely rooms, I play our songs no more,
The garish Sun shines flauntingly upon the unswept floor;
The mocking-bird still sits and sings, O melancholy strain!

For my heart is like an Autumn-cloud that overflows
with rain;

Thou art lost to me forever, Isadore!

Alas! how changed is all, dear wife, from that sweet eve
in Spring,

When first my love for thee was told, and thou to me
didst cling,

Thy sweet eyes radiant through their tears, pressing thy
lips to mine,

In our old arbor, Dear, beneath the over-arching vine;—

Those lips are cold forever, Isadore!

The moonlight struggled through the leaves and fell upon
thy face,

So lovingly upturning there, with pure and trustful gaze;

The Southern breezes murmured through the dark cloud
of thy hair,

As like a happy child thou didst in my arms nestle there;—

Death holds thee now forever, Isadore!

Thy love and faith so plighted then, with mingled smile
and tear,

Was never broken, Darling, while we dwelt together here:

Nor bitter word, nor dark, cold look thou ever gavest me—

Loving and trusting always, as I loved and worshipped
thee;—

Thou art lost to me forever, Isadore!

Thou wast my nurse in sickness, and my comforter in health,
So gentle and so constant, when our love was all our wealth:
Thy voice of music cheered me, Love, in each despondent
    hour,
As Heaven's sweet honey-dew consoles the bruised and
    broken flower;—
        Thou art lost to me forever, Isadore!

Thou art gone from me forever;—I have lost thee, Isadore!
And desolate and lonely I shall be forevermore:
Our children hold me, Darling, or I to God should pray
To let me cast the burthen of this long, dark life away,
        And see thy face in Heaven, Isadore!

CARISIMA.

"DO YOU NOT KNOW I LOVE YOU?"—So you cried,
And blessed my lips with kisses multiplied,
Sweeter than those for which Adonis died—

    Kisses that promised true love's long endurance;
While your dear eyes in mine my soul were reading,
With wistful, anxious, eager question pleading,

        To know if I believed the sweet assurance.

"YES, I DO KNOW YOU LOVE ME,"—I replied,
"And in that love I am beatified;
"It is my wealth, my glory, and my pride,

    "The evening-glory of a clouded west:"—
Without it earth were but a desert dreary,
Under life's burthens I should faint and weary,

    And long to fall asleep and be at rest.

Darling! with what can I such love repay?
What can October give to delicate May?—
The afternoon hours of a waning day,

    The saddening Autumn of Life's fading year.—
I can but give the love that sacrifices
Itself to bless the one it idolizes,—

    Itself, and all delights to lovers dear.

Sad recollections of the shadowy years,
Of radiant hopes fainting to gloomy fears,
Of smiles and laughter dying into tears,
   These, and no more, remain to me of life.
These and no more!—calamities and crosses,
Regrets and griefs, reverses, and the losses
   That were the bitter fruits of civil strife.

Sad memories of lost loves and broken trust,
Kisses from lips long mouldered into dust,
Short lived delights that ended in disgust,—
   These are the only treasures of the Past;
A Past of love, dreams, shadows, mirth and sadness,
Of hours of reason and long days of madness;
   A morning-sky, with clouds soon overcast.

Youth, Beauty, Genius—more than queenly dower;
Over men's hearts a more than royal power;
The certainty of Fame's triumphal hour;
   An hundred worshippers before your throne;—
How can you, rich with these divine largesses,
Value my love, or care for my caresses?—
   And yet you are my darling and my own.

Like dark and rainy days on bitter sands
Or barren moors—long days in foreign lands,
To one who nothing spoken understands,

    If I did doubt your love, my life would be,—
Aimless and hopeless, like a vessel drifting,
Shattered by storm, before the unquiet, shifting,

    Capricious winds, on a dark Northern sea.

Father in Heaven! I thank thee for the gift
Of this dear love, my grateful soul to lift
Out of the depths!—no more I, blinded, drift

    Alone, in darkness, towards the frowning portal
Beyond whose folds no difference of age is,
Where those who love may read the same bright pages,

    In the mysterious Book of Love immortal.

                      April, 1869.

A FRAGMENT.

        Like the young moon,
    When, on the sunlit limits of the night,
    Her white sheen trembles amid crimson air,
    And whilst the sleeping tempest gathers might,
    Doth as the herald of her coming, bear
    The ghost of her dead mother, whose dim form
    Bends in dark ether from her infant's chair.

"LOVE BLOOMS BUT ONCE."

A SONG.

When Autumn's chilly winds complain
  And red leaves withered fall,
We know that Spring will laugh again,
  And leaf and flower recall.

But when Love's saddening Autumn wears
  The hues that death presage,
No Spring in Winter's lap prepares
  A second Golden Age.

So when Life's Autumn sadly sighs,
  Yet smiles its cold tears through,
No Spring, with warm and sunny skies,
  The Soul's youth will renew.

Love blooms but once and dies—for all,—
  Life has no second Spring:
The frost must come, the snow must fall,
  Loud as the lark may sing.

O Love! O Life! ye fade like flowers,
  That droop and die in June;
The present, ah! too short, is ours;
  And Autumn comes too soon.

1865.

MIGNONNE.

In the sad evening of my life,
 A single star upon me smiles,
And makes the world's turmoil and strife
 Seem distant from me many miles,—
The Star of one great love, that gleams
 My solitary way upon;—
I love once more, and in my dreams
 I whisper one dear name—MY DARLING, CHERE
  MIGNONNE!

I love you with a man's great love,
 A loyal love, profound and true,
Pure as the star-light that above
 The low earth loves to shine on you:
A love that all my being fills,
 And cannot wane till life is done,
Whose passionate ardour through me thrills,
 And makes me all thy slave, MY DARLING, CHERE
  MIGNONNE!

No fancy 't is, no mere desire,
  No furious and fickle flame;—
Such love did Petrarch's soul inspire,
  And make immortal Dante's name:—
A love that finds its recompense
  In serving the beloved one,—
So pure, so perfect, so intense,
    My deathless love for you, MY DARLING, CHERE
      MIGNONNE!

Your passionate love I cannot win;
  Life's Autumn cannot be so blest:—
Lock up my secret, Darling! in
  The sanctuary of your breast!
Let none my idle passion know!
  No answering love I count upon,
Yet cannot help but love you so,
    And wish for youth once more, MY DARLING, CHERE
      MIGNONNE!

And if I sometimes chafe, because
  You are indifferent and cold,
And Nature will not change her laws,
  And teach the young to love the old;
I do not love you less, but more:
  Of all the world of women none,
Though I have often loved before,
    Has been so loved as you, MY DARLING, CHERE
      MIGNONNE!

Am I ungenerous?—It is wrong;
  But love that doubts is always so.
I bear the burthen, when the long,
  Still watches of the sad night go
With slow steps by my sleepless eyes,
  While your sweet kisses linger on
My lips, almost like agonies,
    Because I cannot win MY DARLING, CHERE
      MIGNONNE!

O Darling! love me lest I die!
  Let not the cloud between us stay!
One kiss will chase it from my sky,
  And make the dark night joyous day.
You are my love, my life, my all,
  Yet never to be all my own;
For me the leaves of Autumn fall,
    For you the Spring-flowers bloom, MY DARLING,
      CHERE MIGNONNE!

                                        1868.

LINES TO A LADY.

The wind is low as woman's sigh,
    The myriad stars are shining bright,
The pale moon, like a lustrous eye,
    Smiles calmly on the brow of night;
And close beside her beams one star
    Of love, like woman's deep devotion,
Of one shrined thought the worshipper;
    Pouring its mellow light afar,
Mingled with moonbeams, on the prairie's waveless ocean.

All sounds of mortal sense are still;
    The earth is like a weary child,
That, having played and wept its fill,
    Sleeps calmly in the forest wild;
For she, with all her myriad brood
    Of fiery passions, sleeps like heaven;
While not a murmur stirs the wood,
    Or the green prairie's solitude,
Nor over heaven's face one restless cloud is driven.

And moon, and star, and planet shine
    Upon one home of happiness,
Flooding it with a light divine,
    As though they would its inmates bless,
Where, by the night-breeze gently fanned,
    Like giants calmly slumbering,
Old gnarled oaks, a sturdy band,
Around that lonely dwelling stand,
And o'er its roof their wild, grotesque arms fondly fling.

This pleasant night will soon be gone,
    As vanishes a sunny dream;
'Tis but a bubble, floating on
    Old Time's resistless, rapid stream.
Yet shall thy sky, sweet lady, be
    For ever cloudless, clear, and bright,
As this that now I joy to see
In all its glittering mystery,
Over thy home of peace wheeling its rapid flight.

1846.

*THE OLD CANOE.

Where the rocks are gray and the shore is steep,

And the waters below look dark and deep,

Where the rugged pine, in its lonely pride,

Leans gloomily over the murky tide;

Where the reeds and the rushes are long and lank,

And the weeds grow thick on the winding bank,

Where the shadow is heavy the whole day through,

There lies at its mooring the old canoe.

The useless paddles are idly dropped,

Like a sea bird's wings that the storm has lopped,

And crossed on the railing, one o'er one,

Like the folded hands when the work is done,

While busily back and forth between,

The spider stretches his silvery screen

And the solemn owl with the dull "too whoo,"

Settles down on the side of the old canoe.

---

*While the authorship of this beautiful poem has been credited to
Gen. Pike, it has also been denied that he wrote it, and he himself is said
to have stated that the honor did not belong to him but to a young lady,
whose name has never been mentioned, to the knowledge of the editor
of this volume. The verses were republished in the *Gazette* a few years
ago with this reference:

"We do not know from what paper or magazine they were taken, but
the editor of one, while crediting Gen. Pike with its authorship, makes
this note: 'Long before the war the appended simple but charming
verses appeared, without signature or address, in a short-lived paper at
Little Rock, but it was generally understood that the author was Gen.
Albert Pike.' "

The stern, half sunk in the slimy wave,
Rots slowly away in its living grave,
And the green moss creeps o'er its dull decay,
Hiding its mouldering dust away,
Like the hand that plants o'er the tomb a flower,
Or the ivy that mantels the falling tower,
While many a blossom of loveliest hue,
Springs up o'er the stern of the old canoe.

The currentless waters are dead and still,
But the twilight wind plays with the boat at will,
And lazily in and out again,
It floats the length of the rusty chain;
Like the weary march of the hand of time,
That meet and part at the noon-tide chime,
And the shore is kissed at each turning anew,
By the dripping bow of the old canoe.

Oh, many a time with careless hand,
I have pushed it away from the pebbly strand
And paddled it down where the stream runs quick,
Where the whirls are wild and the eddies are thick,
And laughed as I leaned o'er its rocking side,
And looked below in the broken tide,
To see that the faces and boats were two,
That were mirrored back from the old canoe.
But now, as I lean o'er its crumbling side,
And look below in the sluggish tide,

The face that I see there is graver grown,
And the laugh that I hear is a sober tone,
The hands that lent to the light skiff wings,
Have grown familiar with sterner things;
But I love to think of the hours that sped,
As I rocked where the whirls their white spray shed,
Ere the blossom waved or the green grass grew,
O'er the mouldering stern of the old canoe.

GERTRUDE.

Many sweet flowers in the prairie shine,
   And many in the wood;
But the fairest flower of all is mine,
   My darling young Gertrude.
Her hazel eyes so roguish bright,
Filled with her dear soul's radiant light
Her rosy, pouting lips invite
   The long, warm kiss:
And yesterday, at last, I heard
From that sweet mouth the welcome word
   That makes existence bliss:
My promised wife, star of my life,
   My darling young Gertrude!

Many a bird in the prairie sings,
   And many in the wood:
But none whose song so sweetly rings
   As that of my Gertrude:
The happy day draws swiftly near,
When, trusting to my love sincere,
She will become tenfold more dear,—
   That bright, glad day,
When in my loving, loyal arms,
Enfolding all her glowing charms,
   A thousand times I'll say,
"My dear, sweet wife! star of my life!
   My darling young Gertrude!"

1843.

"The sea, the sea!
    It rings as loud, it rolls as free,
As brightly flashes on this shore,
    As where the deep, grave, calm vibration,
From its great heart's green gushing core,
    Washes the footprints of a nation
Of freemen, on New England's shore."

THE SEA-SHORE.

THE SEA, THE SEA!

It rings as loud, it rolls as free,
As brightly flashes on this shore,
    As where the deep, grave, calm vibration,
From its great heart's green, gushing core,
    Washes the footprints of a nation
Of freemen, on New England's shore.

THE WIND, THE WIND!

Its spirit cometh, pure and kind,
Cooling the heated brow of care;
    It sleeps upon the silent ocean,
Watching the storm-wolves in their lair;
    But yet it calms not my emotion:
My sorrows scourge, and I must bear.

THE SUN, THE SUN!

It shines as bright my heart upon,
As in my own dear native land;
    And inland far the snowy mountains,
By morning's crimson lightning fanned,
    Are blazing like ethereal fountains;
Yet lone and desolate I stand.

THE SKY, THE SKY!
    As brightly opens its blue eye,
As on New England's sunny hills:
    Over it snowy clouds are stealing,
With tender, melancholy thrills,
    As over souls and drifts of feeling;—
Its beauty neither soothes nor stills.

    THE WOODS, THE WOODS!
    Their melancholy solitudes
Are deep and silent as at home,
    Chequered with midnight intervening,
'Mid heavy green and purple gloom.
    Alas! still deeper shades are screening
The heart that no sun-rays illume!

    AH, HEART, SAD HEART!
    'Tis thou that dull and heavy art!
'Tis thou that hast nor calm nor peace!
    Nature is beautiful as ever,
But changed thyself; thou changest these:
    Lost happiness returneth never,
Nor hope, nor boyish impulses.

    MY NATIVE LAND!
    Were this but home, it were all grand,
All beautiful.   It is not home:
    The sky, the wind, the waves that shiver
Against the shore, the forest-gloom,
    Whatever makes the heart-strings quiver,
All their vibrations echo "Home."   1833.

A SONNET.

Lo! the calm evening of a stormy life;
   The Sun, unclouded, in the West declining;
Peace at the end of discontents and strife,
   Peace to the heart long for affection pining;
The mellow radiance that October fancies,
   On clouds no longer storm-vext softly shining,
Whose golden splendor on their blue peaks dances,
   And paints with purple glow the silver lining.—
Mine! and, behold, in gentle splendour smiles,
   Over the mountains and brown wilderness,
The Evening Star, among the silver isles,
   Star of the Love my autumn-eve that blesses,
That never changing, its sweet self expresses,
In loving looks, kind words and bashful kisses.

January, 1874.

THE SILVER WEDDING.

A MASQUE.

Personated at Washington, on the 8th of April, 1878.

JAMES ALEXANDER WILLIAMSON:
ANN WHITFIELD GREGORY:
Married April 7, 1853.

DRAMATIS PERSONAE.

Annus Eighteen Hundred and Fifty-three.
Annus Eighteen Hundred and Seventy-eight.

Content, the Nymph	*Autarke.*
Peace, the Nymph	. *Eirene.*
Love, the Nymph .	*Philotes.*
Confidence, the Nymph	. *Pistis.*
Spring .	*Earine.*
Summer	. *Thereia.*
Autumn	*Phthinoporon.*
Winter	. *Cheimon.*

THE SILVER WEDDING.

A MASQUE.

Annus 1853 loquitur.

Ho! Eighteen Hundred Seventy-Eight, what means this
concourse here?

Whereat we are by Father Time commanded to appear,

Your predecessors twenty-five, part of the long array,

Which waits for you to join it, at the close of your brief
day?—

We come from that dim land, the Past, thick-peopled
with dead years,

Which, born with smiles, grew old with cares, and died
with sobs and tears:

We come, as unto aged men the memories come, that
bring

Past joys to give delight, past griefs again the heart to
sting.

Guests welcome or unwelcome we, according as we bear

Remembrances, to Serf or King, of happiness or care,

Of joys or sorrows, weal or woe, of honour or of shame,

For which some glorify the Past some bitterly defame.

VOICES, AFAR OFF.

NORTH—The Past is the Fate of the Present;
        Is a Realm no change that knows;
SOUTH—Is the Lawgiver of the Future,
        The source of its joys and woes;

EAST — The dead Years are diademed Monarchs,
      Whom the Years that come after obey;
WEST — And yesterday is as remote from us,
      As the Stars are far away.

Annus 1878 loquitur.

You bring, as every Year's ghost brings, sad memories
    to all,

Of losses, disappointments, griefs, that rich and poor
    enthrall;

Yet here you and your comrades bring remembrances of
    Content,

Of good deeds done, of virtuous lives, of no days idly
    spent,

Of much to be with pride reviewed, of little to regret,

Of plighted vows unbroken, and of love not weary yet.

You are welcome, Years of peace and war! in this Elysium,
    where

Parents and children cheerfully life's chafing burdens bear;

Thou, Eighteen Fifty-three, who heardst the vows that
    made these one,

And Ye who know how nobly they the work of life have
    done.

You come as witnesses to prove that they have ever been

Fond husband, faithful, loving wife, patient, unvexed, serene;

As witnesses, renewal of those solemn vows to hear;

Though Ghosts, yet guests most welcome at the Silver
    Wedding's cheer.

Annus 1853 loquitur.

Let, then, the Shades of all the dark, sad days,
   That make large part of every dead Year's train,
Of every woe that stings and sin that slays,
   Unto the Past's dark realm retire again!
But let the Shades of Sorrows here remain,
Which, born with patience, blessings proved and gain.
With these blest Shades let those appear that make
   The home a heaven in which they do abide;
Let them here live, nor in all time forsake
   The house by loving memories sanctified.
Come! fair Content, Peace, Love and Confidence,
Sisters of Hope, and born of Innocence.

Come! with the Seasons of the living Year,
   And while these bring gay flowers and golden fruit,
For those who are to many friends so dear,
   Let them not be indifferent or mute,
But with fair wishes kindly spoken bless
Those who so well do merit happiness.

_**_*Here enter, hand in hand, four young ladies, dressed in white, representing CONTENT, PEACE, LOVE, CONFIDENCE; and two representing SPRING and SUMMER, with two men representing AUTUMN and

WINTER; who all enclose the husband, wife and children in a circle; and Spring, Summer and Autumn crown them with wreaths of flowers, and set at their feet baskets of fruit, at the appointed times. *.*.

Loquitur Content.

I am the Nymph CONTENT:—

    I come with treasures in my hands,—

    Not gold nor gems from many lands,

    But tranquil thoughts and gentle words,

    That please like flowers and songs of birds;

    To me the home enchantment owes,

    The flowers that bloom amid the snows,

    The heart's calm ease, to bravely bear

    Reverses, wrongs, and daily care.

    Hear what an English Poet sung,

    In the days when Queen Elizabeth was young.

*.*Some one at a distance reads:

Sweet are the thoughts that savour of Content;

    The quiet mind is richer than a crown;

Sweet are the nights in careless slumber spent,

    The poor estate scorns Fortune's angry frown;

Such sweet content, such minds, such sleep, such bliss,

That make homes happy, ever dwell in this!

The homely house that harbors peaceful rest,

    The cottage that affords no pride nor care,

The modest ways of maidens neatly drest,

    The sweet consort of mirth and music rare

      These make the truest and most lasting bliss;

      A mind content both crown and kingdom is.

Loquitur Peace.

I am the Nymph PEACE:—

There is peace in the lonely cells,
   In the Convent's cloisters grey,
Where, sweet as the chime of the Convent-bells,
   Life calmly glides away.
But better the peace that blesses
   The family in its home,
Where the grey hairs mingle with bright brown tresses,
   And the Young care not to roam;
Where the eyes of one sister are bright,
   And the voice of another is sweet,
And the father reads in the soft still light,
   And the children play at his feet.
The home of a mother's delight,
   The haven of wedded bliss,
A home that is tranquil and gay and bright,
   Even such a home as this.

Loquitur Love.

I am the life of the household,
   The LOVE of the husband and wife,
The love between parents and children,
   The love that is dearer than life.
Eyes by me lighted grow brighter,
   Hearts by me warmed are glad,

Homes where I live are lighter,
  And sorrowing souls less sad.
When the bridal flowers have withered,
  I do not pine away,
My flowers bloom and are gathered
  In November as in May.
They fade not, this home perfuming,
  As they did so long ago
Here they shall still be blooming,
  When Winter brings his snow.

Loquitur Confidence.

I am the Nymph CONFIDENCE:—
  I drive away distrust and doubt,
    That into homes like serpents crawl;
  And jealousy, that coils about
    The heart and turns the blood to gall.
  Mine are the true and loving eyes,
    Through which one looks in on the Soul,
  The loyal troth that Time defies,
    The faith that can mistrust control.
  Here I abide, a constant guest,
    With Peace and Love, and sweet Content;
  By us this home shall still be blest,
    Beyond the reach of accident.

Annus 1878 loquitur.

Now let my seasons four their homage pay,
  Bringing their offerings meet;
First SPRING, a maiden sprightly, blithe and gay,
  With delicate dancing feet;
Then SUMMER, on whose lips departing May
  Pressed kisses long and sweet;
Then AUTUMN, sober-clad in russet grey,
  Then WINTER, white with sleet.

Loquitur Earine, Spring.

When the man was the maiden wooing,
  And life was a troop of bright hours,
I smiled on and favored the suing,
  And crowned them with garlands of flowers.
Again I bring roses and pansies,
  Carnations and hyacinths, too,
Fair typos of all delicate fancies,
  To crown these now wedded anew.

[Giving Flowers.]

White rosebuds and lilies the rarest,
  Camellias, violets blue,
For these, among maidens the fairest,
  Whose eyes are so tender and true.

[Giving Flowers.]

May the world not for them lose its brightness,
  As the years chase each other away,
Nor their hearts lose the innocent lightness,
  That makes them so happy to-day.

Loquitur Thereia, Summer.

When the Spring died, and I was queen,
  Twenty-five years ago,
And the flowers still bloomed, and the leaves were green,
  And the birds sang loud and low,
    The maiden was matron, and home was gay,
    And the hours swift-footed danced away.
To wife and husband I brought fruits then,
  Golden and green and purple and red,
Now flowers and fruits I bring again,
  After so many years have fled.
    Their summer of life is ended,—
    May its memories that remain,
      Of joys and sorrows blended,
    Give more of pleasure than pain.

Loquitur Phthinoporon, Autumn.

When the days in October grow shorter and colder,
  And leaves are crimsoned by frost,
May these friends whom we love, growing grayer and older,
  No days have to count as lost!
May the world still for them be a good world to live in,
  With good in it always to do,
A good world to help and to comfort and give in,
  With praise for the honest and true.

May they be never sick of hope deferred,
    Nor in the field or vineyard toil in vain;
Nor words of kindness be by them unheard,
    Nor thanklessness of children give them pain.

———

Loquitur Cheimon, Winter.

When I, with storm of snow and sleet
    And wind loud-howling reign,
And pavements are icy in every street,
    And rivers rebel in vain,
In the inter-spaces between the storms,
    When the sky is cold and clear,
May these not want the fire that warms,
    And the good old-fashioned cheer!
Nor the good old wishes become but forms,
    "Merry Christmas" and "Happy New Year."
For the Poet has said and sung
    These words, that are wise and true,
"The Old need not envy the Young,
    "The Old need not scorn the new;
"For hearts can be warm when days are cold,
    "And the night may hallow the day,
"Till the heart, though at even-tide weary and old,
    "May rise in the morning gay,   '
    "To its work in the bright new day."

Loquitur Annus 1853.

Thus said the Poet, in the olden time,
When sense not sound builded the stately rhyme,—
"The cottage nestling in the lowly dale,
  "Ill fortune never fears, because so low;
"The anchored mind, dreading no fickle gale,
  "Sleeps safe when Fate doth Princes overthrow;"
    Content still smiles, when portly statesmen feel
    That fear and danger tread upon their heel.

If Fortune frowns and scowls, may that to these work good!
  If Fortune flattering smiles, may it not prove a snare!
May crosses bravely borne, ills patiently withstood,
  And length of peaceful days for new life them prepare!
May hope gild every cloud, Faith make the future bright,
And patience them maintain in quiet and delight;
While, till their changeless love shines into perfect day,
Bravely they hand in hand do walk their homeward way,
And hear, behind the bells in wintry Autumn ringing,
The soft sweet chorus of the loving angels singing.

THE BRIDAL.

Ring, bells! your glad carillons,
   For two fond hearts made one.
The old, old story telling,
   In Paradise begun.

To holy church now cometh
   The soldier with his bride,
Up the aisle gravely pacing,
   Unto the altar side.

Worth against many rivals,
   Wins more than golden fruit:
Grace, virtue, genius, beauty,
   Reward his patient suit.

Queen over hearts long reigning,
   She lays her sceptre down,
One heart must now content her,
   One love be all her crown.

Must we say "Good-bye!" Darling?
   Ah! word so hard to say!
Must we, so long adoring,
   Give you to him, to-day?

Dear heart of child so loving,
  So tender and so true,
Heart that is ever seeking,
  Some generous act to do:

Dear eyes so bright in gladness,
  To loved ones' faults so blind,
So eloquent in sadness,
  When fortune was unkind.

Hands that were never weary
  Of toil for other's sake;
Tongue that with sweet tones pleading,
  Bitter words never spake:

We part with her in sorrow,
  We give her up with tears,
Losing with her the blessing
  Of all the coming years.

Take, then, this gift most precious,
  Be to her kind and true!
And as you guard and keep her,
  May God be good to you!

May 28, 1878.

CAROLINE.

They said that we should meet no more,
  They said she never should be mine,
They swore to see me dead, before
  I should wed Caroline.
But rivers to the ocean run,
  And none can stay their rapid course;
The springs gush upward to the sun,
  With a resistless force;
Man cannot keep fond lips apart,
Nor sever loving heart from heart,
  Nor me from Caroline.

What claims can fetter the fond soul,
  Or bind the pre-determined will?
I left them in their wealth to roll,
  I was a free man still.
I wandered to the far Southwest,
  I labored manfully and long,
For Caroline inspired my breast,
  Her promise made me strong.
And now, a free man still, I ride,
To claim my lovely, blushing bride,
  My dark-eyed Caroline.

There is a green and cheerful spot,
   Where, through a valley, ramparted
With mountains, the bright COSSITOT
   Sparkles along its bed;
The forest, from the river's brim
   In stately semicircle sweeps;
In which, imprisoned like a gem,
   An emerald meadow sleeps;
Across it, through the columned green,
A pleasant cottage may be seen,
   Builded for Caroline.

No earl hath lovlier demesne
   Than that fair valley's solitude;
Nor looks on forests half so green
   As that primeval wood.
And it is honestly my own,
   Its price with my own hands I earned,
For long I labored there alone,
   While still I often turned
Mine eyes to our old home, and knew
That there she waited, fond and true,
   My constant Caroline.

My dear wife's loving, happy eyes,
    Her cheerful voice and sunny looks,
Our love, that flower from Paradise,
    And music, and old books;
With honest labor every day,
    All blessing our sweet solitude,
Shall from our fireside scare away
    All troubles that intrude.
And while life calmly journeys on,
Dearer with each returning sun
    Shall be my Caroline.

1840.

SONG.

The day has passed, love, when I might
  Have offered thee this heart of mine,
As one whose yet unclouded light
  Was clear and pure, and bright as thine.
When, though I gazed on thee as one
  Who worships a bright distant star,
Thou didst not blush to be my sun,
  Mine, dear, thy Persian worshipper.

And now, although it be but shame
  To be adored by such as I,
That love in sadness yet will flame,
  Knows no decay, can never die.
Its soul of fire has no decline,—
  Rocks check not the abundant river;
And though thou never canst be mine,
  I'm thine, love, thine alone, forever.

1832.

"WILT THOU ON THY SWEET BOSOM WEAR?"

Wilt thou on thy sweet bosom wear,
   The cross I send to thee,
Disdaining not the gift that tells
   How dear thou art to me?—
Threads of thy soft, brown, precious hair
   Do therein interwine,
Querida! by thy sweet consent,
   With some gray threads of mine.

Sweetheart! perhaps, when I am dead,
   It may kind memories wake,
Of one who little cares to live,
   Except for thy sweet sake;
Who, hoping for such love alone,
   As youth to age can give,
Could, losing even that, no less
   Only to love you live.

Darling! upon my breast unseen,
  Its match and mate I wear,
Thrilled with the same sweet influence,
  As when thy head lay there:—
And those who find it there when I
  Am silent, still and cold,
May say, perhaps, "this man still loved,
  "Though he was gray and old."

There let them leave the triple cross,
  Of deathless love the sign,
Under the grass and on my heart,
  For it is wholly mine:—
Though frost-sere leaf and soft spring-flower
  Not fit companions be,
Yet I, grown old, O Darling! love
  Beyond all measure thee.

Nov. 13, 1874.

ANNIE.

The golden, climbing jasmine grows
  Along the bright, clear Ouachita:
On each bewildered wind that blows,
Its sweet perfume there overflows,
  And, eddying, floats afar.
It is a wild, sweet, simple flower,
  Each leaf a glossy evergreen,—
And when the spring-rains softly shower,
  Its jewelled ringlets, gold and green,
  Floats on the charmed air, between
  The stately trees, that overlean
    The sunny Ouachita.

Up each tall oak and sturdy ash,
  And elm, along the Ouachita,
Where dew-drops on the thick leaves plash,
Its flowers like beauty's glad eyes flash,
  Each a bright golden star,—
Tempting the mad bees there to roam,
  Great misers, adding to their store
Of honey, in their hollow home,
  In that great branching sycamore,
Around whose knees the waters roar,
  A dozen centuries or more,
    On sunny Ouachita.

I love its simple flowers that gleam
    Along the silver Ouachita:
I love the bright, clear, dancing stream,
For there I dreamed a happy dream,
    Brief, as all such dreams are.
I met my little ANNIE there,
    A dear, sweet, lovely, blushing maid,
A flower as delicate and fair
    As those I twined with each dark braid
    Of glossy hair, while far we strayed,
    Wrapt in the green trees' pleasant shade,
      By sunny Ouachita.

Her soft eyes, and her angel face,
    Like sunshine, blessed the Ouachita:
And blushing in my fond embrace,
With childlike innocence and grace,
    Trusting, she wandered far.
There, hand in hand, and heart in heart,
    Two souls together knit in one,
We lingered daily, loth to part,
    Nor noticed, as the green world spun
    Unceasingly around the sun,
    Time's river swiftly by us run,
      Like rapid Ouachita.

How fondly did her soft arms twine
 Around me on the Ouachita!
Her sweet lips chastely pressed to mine,
Her brown eyes radiant and divine,—
 Each brighter than a star.
She was my heart, my soul, my all;
 I loved her dearer than my life;
And ere the autumn leaves should fall,
 Shorn by the sharp frost's glittering knife,
 I hoped, escaping the world's strife,
 To make her my own darling wife,
  On sunny Ouachita.

Sadly, Ah! sadly by me glide
 Thy waters, clear, cold Ouachita!
My Annie, my betrothed bride,
That summer, sickened, drooped, and died!
 My Heaven lost its star.
A prayer for me was on her lips,—
 The last she ever uttered here;
Her sweet eyes, dark in death's eclipse,
 For me still glittered with a tear:
 Why could I not be with thee, dear,
 Or know that thou wast dying, near
  The sunny Ouachita?

Thy woods are green, thy flowers are bright,
 Thy waters sparkle, Ouachita!
Thy glades still gleam with golden light;
But day to me is like a night
 Moonless, without a star.
Dear Annie! while above thy grave
 I sing this melancholy strain,
The wild-flowers that upon it wave
 Are watered with my eyes' warm rain,
 Yet does one happy thought remain:—
 WE SHALL BE ONE IN HEAVEN AGAIN,
  AS ON THE OUACHITA.

1844.

THE WAIF RETURNED.

I send home your glove, my darling!
  Darling! love and true!
Yester-eve left where you sat by me;
  And my heart goes with it to you.

Goes with it all love and devotion,
  To win sweet looks from your eyes,
Like the flower which, thirsting in Summer,
  For the sweet rain at noon-day sighs.

I send it, yet fain would keep it,
  For the little hand that, in mine,
Yester-eve so lovingly nestled,
  When your kisses were sweeter than wine.

Come back soon!—I pine, my darling!
  For the clasp of your hand again;
Bring back, Dear! the heart that goes to you,
  And struggles for freedom in vain.

August 16, 1875.

THE LIGHT OF DAYS LONG PAST.

Our afternoon of life has come,
　　Its darkening hours are here;
The evening shadows lengthen,
　　And the night is drawing near;
To some the sky is bright, to some.
　　With clouds is overcast;
But still upon our Present smiles
　　The Light of Days long past.

The Autumn of our life is here,
　　Its summer flowers are dead;
But still the wine-cup charms us,
　　And young lips rosy-red.
What though the river to the sea
　　Runs steadily and fast?
Upon its shifting waves still smiles
　　The Light of Days long past.

We meet here as we met of old,
　　Kind words to say or sing;
Forgetting age, and all the cares
　　That age and losses bring:
The friendships sealed in younger days
　　Still firm and faithful last,
And newer friendships brighten in
　　The Light of Days long past.

1866.

FANNY.

Through the broad, rolling prairie I'll merrily ride,
Though father may fume, and though mother may chide,
To the green, leafy island—the largest of three—
That quietly sleeps in that silent, green sea;
For there my dear Fanny, my gentle young Fanny,
My own darling Fanny, is waiting for me.

Ho! Selim! push on!— The green isle's still afar,
And morning's red blush dims the dawn's regal star;
Before the sun rises, she'll watch there for me,
Her eyes like twin-planets that soothe the vext sea;—
My young, black-eyed Fanny, my winsome, sweet Fanny,
My own darling Fanny, will watch there for me.

Swift, Selim! swift, sluggard!—more swiftly than this;
There are ripe, rosy lips that I'm dying to kiss,
And a dear little bosom will throb with delight,
When the star on your forehead first glitters in sight;—
My glad, little Fanny, my arch, merry Fanny,
My graceful, fair Fanny,—no star is so bright.

Then her soft, snowy arms round me fondly will twine,
And her warm, rosy lips will be pressed close to mine,
And her innocent bosom with rapture will beat,
When again, and no more to be parted, we meet:
My lovely young Fanny, my own darling Fanny,
The flower of the prairie, so modest and sweet.

So, father may grumble, and mother may cry,
And sister may scold;—I know very well why;
'Tis that beauty and virtue are all Fanny's store,
That, while we are rich, she, alas! is quite poor;—
My lovely young Fanny, my faithful, true Fanny,
My own darling Fanny, I'll love you the more.

Ho, Selim! fleet Selim! bound fast o'er the plain!
The morning advances, the stars swiftly wane;
I see in the distance the green, leafy isle—
Between us and it stretch full many a mile—
Where my true-hearted Fanny, my own constant Fanny,
Shall welcome us both with a tear and a smile.

1842.

THE HUSBAND TO HIS WIFE.

Thy anguish bosom heaves no sigh,
  So well it can its woes control;
Yet, gentle angel! how thine eye,
  With its calm sadness, racks my soul.

I brought thee from thy happy home,
  To wed with want and wretchedness;
And dost thou to my bosom come,
  And him who made thee wretched bless?

In all but love, how poor we are!
  Yet thou wast cradled, dear, in ease;
And I—forgive me gentle star!
  And bless me with one smile of peace!

And thou art dying!—well, too well
  I see death's mark upon thy brow;
Thine eyes the fatal message tell,
  That I must lose thee, even now,

Dear love! reproach me not! Too hard
  Are now my own stern thoughts to bear;
That I thy happiness have marred,
  And dimmed the jewel that I wear.

Come, sing to me, as thou didst sing,
  Ere life had grown all grief and pain;
Till sorrow to me cease to cling,
  And I become a boy again.

Perhaps we may be happier,
  And yet some days of gladness see;
If not,—ah,—death were welcomer
  Than one reproachful look from thee.

————

THE ANSWER.

Think not, dear husband, that my heart
  Hath ever blamed thee for its pains;
Dearer and closer still thou art,
  As life's short day too swiftly wanes.

'Tis true I left my father's home;
  I left it gladly, love, for thee:
And thou in sunshine and in gloom,
  Hast been the universe to me.

'Tis true that we are poor, too poor,—
  But there's a joy in poverty;
I well knew what we must endure;—
  How can I murmur, then, at thee?

Twine thy loved arms around me, dear!
  Pillow my head upon thy breast;
And while our pitiless fate draws near,
  Let us prepare to take our rest.

And I will sing to thee, the song
  By which my virgin heart was won,
Till thou shalt wander back, among
  Those joys that now, alas! are gone.

So let our poor lives faint away,
  Like the sad cadence of the strain;
And like twin stars at dawn of day,
  Together we will calmly wane.

1833.

HOME.

How many a tongue
With words of wondrous eloquence, hath sung
Of "Home, sweet Home!" How the old memories throng,
Stirred by the sweet notes of the dear old song,
Into the heart, and tears suffuse the eyes,
Of high and low, the simple and the wise.
'Tis a trite theme: and yet if it impart
One new, fresh feeling to the wearied heart,
Why not sing of it, when the sad soul longs
To hear the old, familiar, simple songs?
Old memories that visit us in dreams
Are always most delicious; and old themes
The only beautiful. Whoever hath
No pleasant recollection of the path
He paced to school, of the orchard, the old mill
Clacking and clattering with a rare good will,
The fields and meadows, and the silver brooks
That often made him truant to his books,
The marshes where he shot, the clear cold streams
Where the trout lurks;—who never in his dreams
Drinks from the bucket at the deep old well,
Or in the old church hears the old organ swell;
Hath grown hard-hearted, needs must be unkind,

And deserves pity from the poorest hind.
All things whatever that we see or hear,
Contain Home's image, and to eye and ear
Bring back old things; as in pellucid lakes
The clouds are imaged, when the fresh dawn breaks.
Is it because the heart to the harp is like,
The simple harp, which, on it though you strike
A hundred notes, has still its undertone,
The key-note of them all, that rings alone,
A pensive sound, after the rest are dead?
The fresh cool rain, that plashes overhead,
On the clay-covered roof, the music rude,
Invading suddenly my solitude,
With discord dire, true Aztec minstrelsy,
A barbarous music, murdered barbarously;
The delicate foot that glances past the door;
Bring vividly from memory's lumber-store,
The rains that often lulled me to sweet rest
In the old garret, where I lay and guessed
At the meaning of full many a puzzling book;
The music of the clear contented brook,
That over the pebbles, chafing into foam,
Ran rippling, half a mile or so from home;
The ancient well-sweep, older than my sire,
A stout and hale old age; the warm peat-fire
Of winter nights, when out of doors the sleet
And drifting snow at door and window beat;

The brave old house, fallen somewhat to decay,
Yet sound to the core, lusty, though mossed and gray,
With its dark rafters of good Yankee oak,
Seasoned by time, and blackened by much smoke;
Familiar fields walled round with massive rocks,
Where the autumn-harvest stood in sheaves and shocks;
And every ancient and familiar thing,
That seemed to watch and love me slumbering:
The magic music of my old friend's flute;
So very soft, yet rich, and sound and clear;
Though, sweet as it was, when its fine tones were mute,
His voice was still more pleasant to my ear.
The foot—but that's a dream:—
Yet one may keep alive a sunny dream,
In some green nook, deep in his inmost heart.
Ah! never may that priceless dream depart,
Or, fading, cease life's twilight-hours to bless!
That memory of the love and happiness,
That were the sunlight of life's golden dawn.
As summer-showers to the emaciated lawn;
Dews to sweet flowers; light to the sky-lark's eyes,
Who fain would sing at the gates of Paradise
His orisons, and thinks dawn comes too slow;
Leaves and cool shade to the nested throstle; so
To me that dream of early love is dear,
When frowning DESTINY is most austere;
Even when he chills the soul with cold eclipse,

The memory of long kisses on sweet lips,
The clear brown eyes, the gentle, loving look,
All soothe me, like some melancholy book
Of beautiful words, wherein enraged men read,
Until to passion gentle thoughts succeed,
And, as the book is, they are quiet too.

                                        1832.

ELLEN.

We parted in the Spring,
When the flowers were all in bloom,
When the air was loaded with perfume,
    And birds were on the wing:
Fondly the dear girl I caressed;
To her fair brow my lips I pressed,
Clasping her closely to my breast,
Then turned my sad eyes to the West,
    And left my darling Ellen.

We parted at the spring,
Where first she told her love,
The thick stars shining bright above,
    The waters murmuring.
We were so poor we could not wed,
Lest we and ours should want for bread;
And so my humble sail I spread,
And westward turned my shallop's head,
    To work, and win my Ellen.

She was a young thing then;
Her bright eyes filled with tears:
Her bosom, then disturbed with fears,
    Shall bound with joy again.
At last, my long probation's done;
Four weary years their course have run,

And, fame and fortune earned and won,
I come to my beloved one,
   My true love, my sweet Ellen.

   Ho, Soldan!   Ho, good steed!
This is the last day's ride:
Bear me but safe to Ellen's side,
   And thou shalt rest indeed;
When, smiling through a rain of tears,
She pours in my enraptured ears
Her tale of many hopes and fears,
That haunted her for four long years,—
   My fond, my faithful Ellen.

   Then, parted nevermore,
Our life shall calmly glide,
Like a clear river's tranquil tide
   Along a grassy shore;
Or, if there come some carking care
Between us we'll the burden share,
Making it easier to bear:—
Ho, Soldan! we are almost there!
   Speed on to my sweet Ellen!

1840.

O DEAREST, O DAINTIEST MIGNONNE!

O dearest, O daintiest Mignonne!—
   O Darling! most perfect and rare!—
What one of all Eve's fairest daughters
   With Mignonne can claim to compare?

Your gray eyes take captive your lovers,
   Your kisses are each worth a throne;
Your dear arms and hands would impassion
   A statue of Parian stone.

Your voice thrills with exquisite pathos,
   In every heart that can feel
The magic of song and sweet music,
   And of all that these jointly reveal.

Your lips, curled in scorn, are delicious,
   When you pout, you are lovelier still,—
When they part, as enchanted I kiss them,
   My soul with glad rapture they thrill.

Your bosom—we see but its contour,
   And dream of its beauties divine;
So was Paradise closed against Adam,
   As Love veils his holiest shrine.

Your dear little lily-stem fingers
    Weave nets for the catching of hearts;
Your tresses make fetters to bind them,—
    The slaves of your mischievous arts.

Your little feet make sweetest music,
    Your ankle one's fingers can span;—
What exquisite charms do you hide from
    The eyes of inquisitive man!

My heart struggles hard in your meshes,
    Like a bird in a merciless hand;
I'm your captive, your servant, your bondsman,
    Obedient to every command.

Capricious and willful, but loving,
    Offended, you quickly forgive;
For you know that I love you so dearly,
    I must cease, if you do not, to live.

You smile, Heaven's golden gates open,—
    With light heart all dangers we dare;
You frown,—and the gates shut behind us,
    We sink in the pit of despair.

O dearest, O daintiest Mignonne!
    O Darling! most perfect and sweet!—
On my heart, if you will, you can trample,
    For 'tis under your delicate feet.   1868.

LOVE.

I am the soul of the Universe,
 In Nature's pulse I beat;
To Doom and Death I am a curse,
 I trample them under my feet.

Creation's every voice is mine,
 I breathe in its every tone;
I have in every heart a shrine,
 A consecrated throne.

The whisper that sings in the summer leaves,
 The hymn of the star-lit brook,
The martin that nests in the ivied eaves,
 The dove in his shaded nook,

The quivering heart of the blushing flower,
 The thick Æolian grass,
The harmonies of the summer shower,
 The south wind's soft, sweet mass,

The psalm of the great grave sea,—are mine;
 The cataract's thunder tongue,
The monody of the mountain pine,
 Moaning the cliffs among.

I kiss the snowy breasts of the maiden,
 And they thrill with a new delight;
While the crimson pulses flush and redden,
 Along the forehead's white.

I fill the restless heart of the boy,
 As a sphere is filled with fire,
Till it quivers and trembles with hope and joy,
 Like the strings of a golden lyre.

I touch the poet's soul with my wing,
 It yields to my magic power,
And the songs of his mighty passions ring,
 Till the world is full of the shower.

The heart of the soldier bows to me,
 His arms aside are flung,
Unheeded the wild sublimity
 Of the silver trumpet's tongue.

I brood on the soul like a golden thrush,
 My music to it clings,
And its purple fountains throb and flush,
 In the crimson light of my wings.

Deep in a lovely woman's soul
I love to build my throne,
For the harmonies that through it roll
Are the echoes of one tone.

The sounds of its many perfect strings
Have but one key-note ever,
Its passions are the thousand springs,
All flowing to one river.

1835.

FRAGMENTS.

FROM "THE BRIGAND." A POEM.

"Bring the wine-cup, companions! and let it go round!
At its bottom good humor and mirth will be found;
Bring the cup—we'll drink deep to the spirit of wine,
The true inspiration and nectar divine.

Boy! take round a draught to the brave *Lanzador;*
Ere another sun sets we his loss may deplore.
Pass not the *Tuerto!* His sword is as good
As the best, and has drunken as deeply of blood.

Take the cup to *San Pablo!* He seemeth to wink,—
His saintship has well earned a license to drink;
For his children, the priests, he has oft helped to heaven,
By many a penance and stripe he has given.

No offence to *El Padre!*—oh, no! for his hand
Is acceptable, armed with the cup or the brand:
Drink deep to his health! and whenever we die,
In the camp or the field, may *El Padre* be nigh!

One draught to ourselves! To the League of the Free!
To the band that is feared from the hills to the sea!
Let the proud Viceroy fume! we his thunders defy,
And his treasures we confiscate under his eye.

The panther-trod mountains encircle our camp,
We descend like the wind at our bold leader's stamp;
And who would exchange the free life that he leads,
For the patter of prayers, and the counting of beads!

Drink deep to our captain, the brave and the true!
To the heart that chill fear and weak parley ne'er knew!
To him whose black plume, and the flame of whose brand,
Are watchwords of terror and fear through the land.

Valverde!   Valverde!—The pale cowards quake,
And the rock-walled cities and fortresses shake,
When his name rings around like the roar of the sea;—
Valverde!   Valverde!   The Sword of the Free."

Such was the song that foamed along the rocks,
And echoed from the thunder-rifted blocks,
In many tongues.   Such was the festal song
Of the Bandits.

               The rugged cliffs among
They had their camp.   On every side uplifted
Preciptious mountains, hoary with white foam sifted
Eternally upon their barren crowns,
Forever braving the fierce Storm-God's frowns,
And the Sun's laugh.   No foot, in all the time
Since the world's making, had essayed to climb
The mountains there, so steep and rough were they.

And here, encircled so on all sides, lay
Sleeping within, an oval, verdant vale,
From which descended but one narrow trail,
A rocky pass, leading to where, below,
The plains spread out;—and through that crooked pass,
Fed in the vale by fountains brimmed with grass
And golden flowers, a silver streamlet ran.
The mountain-breezes never failed to fan
That narrow pass, and that most fertile vale.

The sun was down; but heaven had not grown pale,
For over it there flushed the million hues,
In rainbow cradles, out of the misty dews.
Here, on the summits of far-reaching hills,
The snow was stained with all those sunset thrills;
And there, thick-shaded, had a dim and gray
And misty look, as though dusk Eve did stray
Before her time, out from her eastern cave.
Around the mountain-bases thick did wave
Funereal firs; and in the vale there stood
A haughty and magnificent old brood
Of giant pines.
                    Watch-fires around were built,
And here and there stood, leaning on the hilt
Of his good brand, a bearded sentinel,
Stern and immovable, while thickly fell
The shouts of revelry upon his ear.
Caution was there, although no sign of fear:

And if the eye glanced round among the crags,
It might perceive, behind projecting jags,
Dark forms, half-hidden, all along the pass,
Still as though portions of the mountain-mass.
Here stood a lance, there lay a spotted blade
Upon the sod,—plain emblems of the trade
Of those who revelled; each of whom yet wore
His pistols in his belt; while, close before
A watch-fire, stood some bulky stacks of arms,
Ready for grasping by the owners' palms.
Some, massive muskets of the Tower stamp,
And some the truer rifle.   Through the camp,
There was an air of watchful discipline,
Most stern and strict; such as is rarely seen
With those who have no law but their own will.

Above, and where the narrow, flowering vale
Grew narrower, and where a shifting sail
Of mist was floating up among the rough
And rugged branches of the giant trees;
And where a tall, gray, overhanging bluff
Gave shelter to the dim obscurities,
That cowered beneath, dreading the evening breeze,
Sat the stern chief.   A broad and gnarled root
Lent him a seat, where, at the mountain's foot,
He rested, hearing not the shouts below,
Wherewith the winds were burdened, that did blow,

Drowning the voice, murmuring and musical,
Of the swift brook and slender waterfall,
That babbled near him, fed by faithful springs,
And by cold waters, dropping from the wings
Of crystalled snow.   He had let fall his head
Upon his hands, as though he sadly fed
His memory with almost forgotten dreams,
Or winged Hopes, wherewith the Fancy teems.
And so he kept, until the crimson flush
Had vanished, at the Night-God's westward rush,
And the still stars began to tread the sky,
With their white feet, desiring to espy
The gentle moon in the far orient.
Why was the chieftain, like an old man, bent?
Why shook his frame with many a stifled sigh?
Why paled still more that pallid face?   His eye,
Why is it dimmed with tears that will not fall,
As if the tenderness that unto all
Will cling, though far within the deepest nook
And inmost chambers of the dark heart, shook
His form, and raised the warm dew from his heart
Into his eyes?

        When night and day did part,
Lingerlingly, on the occidental marge,
And the sweet moon her silver orb did charge
With the sun's love; and shyly lifting not
Her eye, as yet, up from the shadowy grot

Behind the mountains, still shot up her spirit
Over their crowns, and the fair Star of Love,
Like some ethereal boat, when angels steer it,
Beamed brilliantly through the tall, gloomy grove
Of graceful firs that crowned the western hill;
Like a clear beacon set upon blue waves
To lighten sailors' hearts that fear cold graves;
He seemed to wander in the tangled maze
Of his own thoughts, as in a wilderness,
And on the glories of the Heavens gaze,
Like one who looks at things, but nothing sees,
Mingling them all in one misshapen blot;
Or, if he sees them, making them a part
Of the one thought, on which the burning heart
Is all concentered, till it is all thought.

There is an old walled city standing near
The broad Pacific's curving, sandy verge;
Whose very walls are sometimes, by the surge,
Whitened with foam.   Great palaces are there,
That glitter in the clear Peruvian air;
And grand cathedrals, with old towering spires,
Reflecting from gold ornaments the fires
Of the eternal sun.   Along the streets
By day and night without cessation beats
The pulse of life, and flows the living tide,
Of pomp and poverty, and woe and pride.

There shaven monk and proud Hidalgo walk,
Or roll in state; and like the lamp-eyed flock
Of Houris that in Paradise are met
By all who truly worship Mahomet,
Fair women congregate, of pleasant eves,
When the bland sea-breezes stirs the orange leaves,
With delicate ankles, round, full, graceful forms,
And eyes as deeply black as midnight storms,
Lighted by lightning; and a gait that shames
Old Andalusia's slender-footed dames.
On all sides of the city, far and near,
Tall mansions, rich with Spanish pomp, appear;
And promenades, o'erarched with flowering trees,
Dropping their blooms at every passing breeze,
Or bent with olives.   All the air is sweet,
For the light sea-winds, with their fairy feet,
Go in and out the honeyed orange-blooms,
And through the thick pomegranates, purple glooms,
Becoming partners with the thievish bees,
In bearing off rich odors.
                    Here was born
Ramon Valverde.   Ere his head had worn
The weight of seven summers, he was sent
To gain, upon the mother continent
An education from her ponderous tomes,
And giant intellects, amid the homes
        Of his dead ancestors, in fair Seville.
His name was not Valverde then; he bore

A prouder name and title, now no more.

There passed some dozen years, while he did fill
His brain with knowledge, such as few obtain,
And then his father called him home again.

Just when his youth bordered on manhood, ere
One hope, one spark of confidence had fainted
In his young soul; while every sense was painted

With golden hues, he left Seville the fair,
And crossed the ocean to his native land,
Glad on the well-known shores once more to stand.
He stood there at the season when the soul
Is most impassioned; when the brilliant goal
Of hope looms up and seems within our reach;
Ere yet experience has begun to teach
His bitter lessons to the wounded heart:
Ere Time has chilled one feeling, in the mart

Of ruined hopes and shattered destinies.
Just at the time when that strange prism, romance,

Lures the glad soul to sunny reveries,
And makes life seem to youth's bold, ardent glance,

All happiness and joy: When Faith and Trust
Have lost not one of all their sunny plumes;

Before the generous nature has been cursed
With dark suspicion, or the frowning glooms
Of stern misanthropy.

Thus was Ramon:
And when he stepped his native shore upon,

His father was a bankrupt.   Men whom he
Had trusted as true friends, had ruined him.
        Alas! this friendship and this treachery!
How many an eye doth perjured friendship dim!—
It is the fortune of the honest man
To trust and be deceived.   It almost seems
Wiser to float upon the troubled streams
        Of the world alone, and give and ask no aid.
Who has not, at some season of his life,
        Had hollow friends and false hearts to upbraid?—
Delayed by storms, Ramon did just arrive
In time to embrace his father while alive.
There was an age in that one parting grasp:
He watched his parent's last convulsive gasp,
And buried him, and mourned him many a day.
Thenceforth he struggled on his lonely way,
Friendless and poor.   Men coldly looked him down:
For 'tis a virtue in the rich, to frown
Upon the poor, and keep him underneath:
It is beneficence to let him breathe
The same good air as they, and tread the soil
Which they tread daintily.
                              In constant toil
And wrestling with his fate, Ramon bore up
A year or two, nor murmured at the cup
Of bitterness.   'Twas very hard for one
Whose spring was brilliant with a cloudless sun,

Full of romance, high hopes and splendid dreams,
Proud, ardent feelings, generous impulses,
To be thus dealt with.

─────────────

One starry night,
He told his love.

─────────────

The young Ramon upon Antonia gazed,
As one might on an angel, that could give
Him immortality.   He did not live
Beyond her presence; for his other life,
Out in the world, was but an evanescene,
A dream of pain and care, of toil and strife,
Lit with the image of that lovely presence,
That peopled his lone heart, and made its cold,
Dark desert once again a Paradise.
So gazing into her deep earnest eyes,
As I have said, his tale of love he told,
Weaving all thoughts, all wishes, all desire,
All hopes and passion into words of fire,
That fell upon her heart, with the intense
Appealing power of love's own eloquence,
And would have won her, had her heart not been
His own already.

There, amid the green
And living foliage of the sleeping trees,
Their faith was plighted.   While the impassive stars,

─114─

With their eternal calm monotony,
Seemed the soul's echo, deeply, fervently,
They vowed to be each other's evermore;
A sacred vow, Heaven's primal shrine before.
How long and happy their sweet conference
Of loving words, or of that most intense
And eloquent silence which is only known
To Love and his young votaries! From her throne
The waxing moon had gone before they parted,
Each to delicious slumber, each light-hearted,
Bouyant with hope. Thence forward, day by day,
Their love grew more intense. When morning gray
Awoke, he found her at the window, reading,
And when pale Eve the flowers with dew was feeding,
She still was there, watching to see his form
Among the busy and incessant swarm
That filled the street. She lived in him alone;
He was her life, a twin-soul to her own:
And when to Heaven she kneeled at twilight dim
And sung her matin song or evening hymn,
To Mary Queen, be sure the words of it
Breathed from *his* soul, and by *his* pen were writ.

Too soon
This dream of hope and happiness was broken:
It would have been by far too great a boon,
For Alvarez, the wealthy, pious-spoken,

Proud Hijo d'algo, to have given to one,
Poor as Ramon, his daughter.   For the son
Of an old noble wooed her, through her sire,
And had his promise.   Then the latent fire
That slumbers in the meekest bosoms woke,
And a new spirit in Antonio spoke
In resolute accents.   She declared her love,
And gloried in 't, and vowed by Him above,
That neither prayers nor force should make her wed,
Save with Ramon, to whom her faith was plighted,
While life remained, unless her reason fled,
And she became like one that gropes, benighted
Along the terror peopled waste of senseless dreams.

Henceforth Ramon was persecuted.   He
Was represented by the priests to be
A favoror of things heretical.
Stoutly they toiled, bribed to effect his fall,
And to the councils did accuse the youth,
As one who was no votary of the truth,
But loved strange doctrines, and had learned to hate
The true belief, endangering the State.
By perjury the miscreants gained their ends;
The poor have seldom very many friends;
And he was soon condemned.

They chained him there,
And gave him to their alguazils to bear
Into the mountains three-score leagues or so,
And leave him on the rocks or frozen snow,
Bound hand and foot, to live as best he might,
Or die and feed the wolves. So did they write
Their stern decree. It fell upon his ear,
But stirred no nerve. He shed no womanish tear,
When 'twas pronounced, or when, next day, he took,
Before they bore him off, his last long look
At the proud palace where his love was kept
As in a cloister; for his eyes had wept
Their last tear now. That was the hour that changed
His inmost nature. That short hour estranged
From him all tender feelings that before
Had fluttered in his heart. The blow that tore
His hopes away, gave him a heart of steel;
Thenceforth he hardly knew what 'twas to feel.
He had been gentle and affectionate,
Most bounteous, though but limited of late,
A shy and modest boy, a genial man;
And his warm blood, although it swiftly ran,
Still throbbed with sympathy, whene'er distress
Called for relief, or wrongs required redress.
But from that hour his heart became austere,
And cold and stern: no passion thence was dear,
Except revenge.

One windy afternoon
In chilly autumn, when the full red moon
Stood on the ramparts of the hills, to gaze
At the veiled sun, just setting in thick haze,
They flung Ramon down on the rocky slope
Of a bleak mountain, and rode swift away,
Leaving him, like a helpless clod, to cope
With death and his despair; and so he lay,
While they rode off with many a jeer and jibe,
The common fashion of the vulgar tribe.
And so he lay, silent and speechless, there,
On the wild sky fixing a steady stare
Of utter hopelessness.   The sun dropped down,
As a torch is quenched.   Night came with heavy frown,
And the gray haze grew thicker in the west,—
Sure indication that the restless ocean
Had sent forth tempest from his teeming breast,
To lash the winds and waters to commotion.
An hour or so the red moon labored through
The heavy masses of gray cloud that grew,
Weltering like billows, over the angry sky,
Until these surges, running mountain-high,
Broke over her, and hid her struggling form,
As when a vessel founders in a storm.
The winds awoke and madly reeled about,
Shrieking amid the cedars, driving out
The hidden darkness from the deepest caves,

To cover the sky: like great engulfing waves,
The fir trees roared and rocked; blue lightning flashed,
Licking the dark crags with its fiery tongue,
And on the cliffs the awful thunder crashed,
And, echoing, to the precipices clung
With a moaning roar. And then the rain broke out,
The sharp white hail, and the great waterspout,
Hurling the rocks down. Swollen rivers bounded
Rejoicingly from crag to crag, surrounded
By crashing trees that fell in splinters there.
Yet he lay helpless. The electric glare
Blinded his eyes; the white hail cut to his bones;
The thunder mocked his agonized moans;
And the storm lulled only to rave again.
The scared wolves, issuing from cave and den,
Blinded with fear, howled loudly as they ran;
And eagles flew so low, their wings did fan
His wounded face. All night the mighty Storm
Haunted the mountains; but his eyeless form
Fled when the sun rose. Dimly, in a cloud
That veiled his brightness like a great, black shroud,
He rose; but soon his fiery, flashing rays
Melted the mist, and then his potent blaze
Became a torture;—so that, all that day,
And its chill night, Ramon despairing lay.
The next day came, with thirst, desire of death,
And restless dozing,—dreams of drinking seas,

Parched tongue, sharp headache, strained eyes, feverish
    breath,
And horrible pangs and spasms; and, by degrees,
Frenzy and madness.   So that day crawled by,
And cold Night came with all her icy stars,
Radiant with freezing splendor in the sky,—
Dear to the sailor, when his shattered spars
Sweep by the Orkneys or bleak Hebrides,
Or where into mountains the salt waters freeze,
By the stormy Cape, or Straits of Magellan.
That night passed also.   Morning came again,
And with it madness.   Then he bruised and beat
His head against the rocks, and tried to eat
His wasted arms, and then would lie and smile
At his poor mangled limbs; and all the while
The hot sun scorched his maddened brain away.
Another night of frost! and then, as day
And sunrise came again, his feeble breath
Flickered upon his lips, and, chilled by Death,
The current of his blood stood still, and he
Lost all sensation.   There some robbers found
What seemed a lifeless body.   Two or three
Passed on and left him; but a stifled sound,
A faint, low grasp, scarce heard, induced one young,
Compassionate novice, to whose soul still clung
Some feeling of humanity, to pour
Wine in his mouth; and then he ran, and bore
From a cold running spring a draught of water

In his broad hat. His eyes unclosed once more;
And, though their trade was robbery and slaughter,
They raised him, fed him, bore him to their camp.
Who shall say wherefore? Ruffians of their stamp
Will do such things at times. They thought, perchance,
Thus to atone for some of their huge crimes;
For, after they had plied the sword and lance,
They told their beads, and chanted pious rhymes.

So life's book opened at another leaf.
Of his preservers he became the chief:
And soon his energy increased the band,
For many joined Valverde the Brigand.
Woe to the priests that met him in the way!
Small time he gave them to repent or pray;
Until his name into a war-cry grew,
Known, hated, dreaded, throught all Peru.
For four long years he had pursued this trade,
And still victorious shone his flashing blade;
Prompt to resolve, and fitted to command,
Ready to plan, and readier his quick hand;
Cautious and bold, and wakeful as a deer,
He ruled his subjects less by love than fear.

Love's white star was down
Behind the hills, when slowly he returned,
And reached the camp. The watchfires brightly burned,

Casting their flickering light upon the trees,—
Those great, grim giants,—and upon the seas,
Of darkness-haunted element above.
And still the sentries through the pillared grove
Paced their slow rounds. White tents the trees amid
Gleamed in the torchlight, half in shadow hid,
And brooding on the grass; and here and there
Were rows of huts, built of great limbs of pine;
And one huge tent blazed with the brilliant glare
Of a great light, where merriment and wine
Flashed into shout and song,—a canvas house,
Vast as a palace, where the band carouse.
Valverde was attracted by the din,
And, flinging back the folds, went calmly in.
From tree to tree the snowy canvas spread;
And silver lamps, swinging far overhead,
Fed with perfume from Cathay and Cashmere,
Flooded with light the mountain-atmosphere.
Round one great table thronged a hundred faces,
Stamped with the characters of many races,
Dark-bearded visages, stern, resolute;
The stout old veteran, and the young recruit.
All was rude splendor: massive plates of gold,
Which hoarding monks long since had ceased to hold
Rich furniture of every costly wood,
Paid for with robber's price, the owner's blood;
Old tapestry of Spain; great gorgeous vases

Of lapis-lazuli and emerald made to hold
Old wine of Xeres; bottles of beaten gold,
Wrought by quaint hands, embellished with saints' faces;
Tall crucifixes gleaming with costly stones;
Great piles of cushions, softer than kings' thrones;
Casks of old wine, bought for the sacrament,
But lost upon the way; rich armor, sent
By curious artisans to holy shrines,
Now swinging from unconsecrated pines;
Chains of gold beads, taken from devotees,
Now ornamenting sacriligious trees;
Cups made of solid agate, for the lip
Of holy abbot, whence the robbers sip
The sacred vintage;—everything, in short,
Which art had made and ample wealth had bought,
Was heaped in strange confusion all around.

The wild, reckless rhyme,
With its quaint words of old Castilian,
That so Valverde chanted, hardly can
Be well translated in our rougher tongue;
But something so it ran:

Up with the Crescent!   Away to the hills!
    We'll die, or save Granada,
The virgin moon her first horn fills,
Her purest light from heaven distills
    On the city, as if to guard her.

Away! away! ere the bloody spray
 Pour into our fastness by rock and crag;
Ere the fiery Cross its wild brilliance toss,
And blaze on our hills while inertly we lag,
 At the ramparts of Granada.

Up, up with the Crescent!   If we are to die,
 To die, or save Granada,
Two lives for one! be our battle-cry;
Each ounce of blood with a pound they shall buy;
 We will fight, and die the harder.
Up, up, and on!   Let the rising sun
 See each a corse or a conqueror!
Up, spear and shield!   The loud cymbal has pealed,
And 'tis time for Mahomet's sons to stir,
 From the ramparts of Granada.

On, on with the Crescent!   The Christians come,
 They think to reach Granada;
And over the rocks to the beat of drum,
We hear their tramp and their busy hum;
 Hush! silence! but on with ardor!
Now, sons of heaven, let their ranks be riven!
 Revenge!   Revenge!   Do ye know the word?
Fight now like men, and the Crescent again,
Like the flap of the eagle's wing, shall be heard
 From the ramparts of Granada.

Canto II.

The silver horn of the advancing tide
Had ploughed its highest furrow in the sand,
And was retiring.   Noon, with hasty stride,
Had passed by forest, beach, and rocky strand,
And golden City, and was on the sea,
Journeying westward.   Every leafy tree
Began to cast long shadows to the east,
And from old Ocean's quiet, deep blue breast,
The evening breeze was lifting more and more,
And slowly drifting toward the longing shore.
The sea-fowls lay, like orbs of silver foam,
On the still surface of their hollow home;
And from the deep transparent element,
Like spiritual echoes faintly went
A slow, sad, plaintive psalm, as if it moaned
To the absent stars, and the great sun enthroned
In the empyrean, and its waves had tongues.
In the blue distance lay some misty throngs
Of green isles sleeping on the emerald sea,
Loveliest of Nature's delicate jewelry.
And one great solitary monument
Of the old fires that shook the Continent,
A thunder-shattered peak, shot up afar,
With snowy head that glittered like a star,
Towering above the ocean.   Toward the shore
White sails now glided, running free before

The freshening breeze; and, anchored firm and fast,
Great ships their lengthening shadows landward cast.
The nautilus came up, and spread his sail
Proudly awhile before the gentle gale,
And then sank down like a dissolving dream,
Or bubble breaking on a dimpled stream.
Just at the edge of these voluptuous seas,
Ran a green pathway, canopied by trees,
Winding in labyrinthine intricacies,
With nooks amid gray trunks, and open spaces
Where lovers could retire, beneath thick vines
And drooping branches, from the common sight,
And breathe their vows.   The rich fruits now were bright
With the sun's spirit, and the grass was green,
Abundant, level, and luxuriant,
And slightly now swept wavingly aslant
By the voluptuous sea-breeze, that began,
Breathing from ocean's cooler bosom, to fan
The forehead of old Tellus, and shake down
The pulpy fruit from the encumbered crown
Of ancient trees, upon the flowery sward.
The sun was slowly verging oceanward,
And, braving now his eye, the dusky shades
Began to gather shyly underneath
Continuous trees.   Here amorous, star-eyed maids,
Like lilies floating on blue lakes, enwreath
Their shapely arms, clustering in merry bands,

And interlocking their small, delicate hands,
With tempting looks from the mantilla glancing,
And little feet that never cease their dancing.
And many a one clings to her lover's side
Alone and trustingly, and some even hide
Themselves in natural grots of twisted vines,
Or of great trees that join their ponderous spines,
There listening to and whispering vows of love,
While ever and anon their bright eyes rove,
To see if any watch the stolen kiss,
And the succeeding blush.

                    In the abyss
Of apathy and care which men call life,
   Who hath not passed such hours? Who looks not back
Through long, dull days, and sleepless nights, and strife,
   To such sweet hours? Who doth not sometimes track
The pathway of the past, and once more stand
Between life's gates, with Memory hand-in-hand,
And feel that one such dear, delicious hour
Outweighs the rest of life? The heart will cower
With shame, regret, sadness, remorse, and pain,
When Memory calls back other hours again;
That one alone is like a pleasant dream
Long vanished, yet more exquisite. We seem
To catch a faint glimpse of a former life,
Among the stars, before our exile here.

Many of these fair maids had tried in vain
To see the face of one who mutely leaned
Against a gnarled old tree, and partly screened
With his full Spanish cloak, his countenance;
And one that somewhat nearer did advance,
A laughing girl, and merrier than wise,
Was so rebuked by his deep mournful eyes,
She shrunk away, abashed.

There came a gentle, almost noiseless step,
Pressing the green grass softly as the lip
Of virgin love.   A fair young girl it was,
With slow and painful gait, and frequent pause,
As if from sickness feeble.

From his face
The dark cloak dropped;   a moment more he stood
Irresolute; then with quick footsteps strode
After the maiden.   Wearied, she had stopped,
Leaning against an orange tree, that dropped
Its blossoms on her hair.   She rose to fly,
With a faint cry of terror; but her eye
Timidly looked in his, her forehead flushed,
Her sweet lips parted, and at once she rushed
Into his arms; her single cry, "Ramon!"
The big tears rained from his full eyes upon
Her wan white cheek and forehead, as he pressed
Her slender form to his broad manly breast,

Her soft eyes closed, and fainting quite away,
Like a fair child upon that breast she lay.
But soon with kisses he brought back her life,
Calling her his angel, his delight, his wife;
And, sitting on a rustic chair, long gazed
On her dear face, till she her sweet eyes raised,
And murmured once again his treasured name,
And kissed his forehead, and his eyes, and laid
Her head again upon his breast, and said,—

"They told me thou wast dead, and I
Believed the cunning, cruel lie.
They said the priests had borne thee, bound
To where the gloomy mountains frowned,
And left thee there, alone, to die;
To watch the dial of the sky
Measure thy fleeting hours of life;
To feel the keen and glittering knife
Of cold hail piercing to thy bones,
And fear to utter dying moans,
Lest to the fierce wolves thou shouldst call.
They told me this; they told me all
That cunning taught them would avail
To render plausible the tale,
I longed to seek thy poor remains,
But like a prisoner in chains,
Within my room was I confined,
Until for want of air I pined,

And wasted to a shadow there.
Like the pale flowers that, growing where
Light never ventures, in deep caves,
Above which thunder the hoarse waves,
Have neither color, scent or hue,
Thus pale, and weak, and faint I grew;
And then they brought thy mouldering bones,
The liars said so, from the thrones
Of storm and snow; and with a din
Of joy and triumph flung them in
The depths of the eternal sea.
And then they once more set me free.

But thou art greatly changed too.   Yet
Thy pale cheeks with fresh tears are wet."

"'Tis true, Antonia, I have wept;
The fountains that so long were dry,
Have overflowed once more, and I
Am young again.   Thine eyes still shine
Upon my own, thy lips kiss mine,
And our past agonies now seem
Only a half-remembered dream.
The heart has many mysteries,
For thou hast lived to taste new bliss
If it be life, indeed, to crave
A sanctuary in the grave;

To loathe the dawn and hate the sun,
As I did, as thou must have done.
I thought thy woman's heart would break,—
I know not why it has not broken,
With grief, despair, and woe unspoken.
For me, I had a thirst to slake,
Within that deep and burning lake,
Revenge, which would not let me die."

"Ah, dear Ramon!" she said, "shall I
Love thee again?   We will not part,
Will we, Ramon?   'Twould break my heart.

Promise; and I no more shall feel
The sickness that so long doth steal
My life-blood and my life away.
Let us not part!   Thou canst not stay
Here, in a city where thy head,
For ancient wrong, hatred half-fed,
And villainy's continual fear,
If thou didst openly appear,
Would make a traitor's fortune.   No!
Better the mountains and cold snow,
Better a frail canoe at sea,
Than danger, doubt, and treachery.
My stern, cold father entertains
All his old hatred; and the rains
Will sooner melt the dark basalt,

Than thou convince him of his fault,
Or soften him. Oh, let us flee
To some far island in the sea!
From care and pain and sorrow part,
Grow strong as giants at the heart,
With happy days and nights of love;
Build up our house in some thick grove;
And live as lovers lived of old.
Then in my arms will I enfold
And press thee, love; will watch thine eye,
And when thou sighest, I will sigh,
Will kiss thine eyes to placid sleep,
And danger from thy slumbers keep;
In life will I be always near,
Nor will I murmur, love, or fear
Cold Death himself. We'll die together,
Like clouds that melt in summer weather:
The gentle wind and summer sea
Shall sing our dirge."

CANTO III.

The twenty-fifth had come; Peru awoke;
One cry for freedom from her green hills broke,
From her wide plains and valleys; and the ocean
Re-echoed it. It was the first emotion
And pulse of her young heart, for LIBERTY.

Oh, holy Freedom! When, ah, when, will be
Thy triumph everywhere? When will the moan
Of the chained nations cease? When will there groan
No slave beneath the broad expanse of heaven?
When will all fetters of the oppressed be riven,
And Tyranny flee, howling, to the caves
Of the bleak mountains; or the mighty waves
All vestige of old slavery overwhelm?
When wilt thou sit, fair Freedom! at the helm
Of the whirling earth, and steer that mighty bark
Now manned by mariners austere and dark,
With cruel eyes, and wearing golden crowns,
Through the wild seas of chaos, where the frowns
Of savage clouds cast shadows on the waves,
Threatening the sailors with unwelcome graves?
Beneath those waves will then be seen the ruin
Of thrones and dominations, there bestrewing
The sandy floor of that engulfing sea,
Peopled with Fear, mad Terror, Agony,
And guant Destruction; steering over which,
Into calm bays and golden seas, will reach
The winged bark, where her storm-shattered sails,
No more will front the lightnings and the gales
Of tyranny and Kinghood. When! oh, when?—
'Tis sad to read the history of men,
And of men's strife for freedom,—see them rise
    From the black gulfs of slavery, and flash
The lightnings of their anger in the eyes

Of trembling kings;—perhaps their tyrants dash,
Bleeding, beneath their feet, amid the crash
Of Bastilles and great palaces; and then
Sink like a wave to anarchy again.
Greece once was free;—how long? Rome, too, that wrote
Her name upon the front of nations, smote
Barbarian empires with unsparing hand,
And bent the world's will to her stern command.
Venice and England, France and Spain, in turn,
Have seen the golden fires of freedom burn.
On hill and plain, on rock and citadel;
In their large light have seen great armies swell,
And dash against the troops of Tyranny.
How often have these waves of Freedom's sea
Been baffled and born back? How often has
Some stern avenger of the People's cause
On Depotism and Kings, himself become
A sterner lord! How often, from the foam
Of tumult and commotion, red with blood,
Some one has risen to ride the furious flood
Of the roused people's rage! How often hath
Some foreign tyrant, mighty in his wrath,
Swept quite away the ramparts of the free,
And trampled them to dust! Dost thou not see,
Oh, Freedom! In thy scroll of bloody names,
Of tiger-hearted men, whose fearful fames

Were from thy children won, wet with thy tears,
PHILIP and CÆSAR, CROMWELL, and that man,
Mightier than all, the wondrous CORSICAN!
Futurity! hast thou a scourge like these
In store for us?   Are stern Fate's dark decrees
Implacable?   The cowering tiger-fiends
Are muttering even now, like restless winds,
Within the dim abysses where they brood,—
Tyranny, Priestcraft, Anarchy, and Feud;
And ever and anon they turn and writhe
Like agonized serpents, long and lithe,
Pressed down by mountains.   Even now the storm
Of discontent is gathering in the warm
And sunny South.   Great clouds the orient clasp,
Rearing their stormy crests, where the white asp
Of lightning quivers, angrily alive:
Freemen are seen too willingly to dive
In the accursed gulf of frantic treason, while
The foes of liberty recline and smile
Within the shadows of old hoary thrones,
Lulled by the music of starved paupers' groans.
Oh, holy Freedom! leave not yet our bark
To drift without a pilot on the dark
And stormy seas of anarchy, and then
To sink forever from the pleasant ken
Of these fair skies and sunny fields, to the home
Of nations tyrant-wrecked, states overthrown,

Republics self-slain! Our great fathers bled
And died for thee, and thy high altar fed
With the red incense of their own stout hearts;
And ere our rights are sold in the black marts
And dens of tyranny, there yet are left
Many to die for thee and thy dear gift.

The cause which made Leonidas eterne,
Embalming his great name within the urn
Of the world's heart,—which made Miltiades,
Pelopidas, and Hampden, and of these,
The twice ten thousand brothers, through all time
Immortal in stern annal and sweet rhyme,—
This cause aroused, and fired all young Peru.
The banner of the LIBERATORS threw
Its eagle shadow on the sunburnt plain,
Now peopled by a small but warlike train
Of Freedom's children. BLAS was there, with some
Five hundred men. BERNAL had left his home
Amid the mountains, with eight hundred more;
BARBON and GOMEZ to the plain did pour,
Each with his gallant regiment, of old
And veteran Catalonians, firm and bold.
ALVAREZ brought a thousand men, a part
Bold mountaineers, skilled in the hunter's art,
A part stout husbandmen, that tilled the plains,
And some old veterans who had stood through rains
Of lead and iron 'gainst Napoleon.

With them had also gathered many a one
Of smaller note; and, in the whole, the force
Amounted to five thousand, foot and horse.
PEPINA still was absent, and the band
Held in the mountains by the brave BRIGAND;
And long and anxiously through all that day,
The leaders looked to see him make his way
Into the plain;—vainly!—for until night
Nothing of him or his appeared in sight;
And when the stars near the young moon were met,
And round the camp the sentinels were set,
Still no troops came, and nothing more was known,
Except that he had failed them; haply, thrown
His weight into the Viceroy's serried ranks,
To obtain thereby pardon, perhaps, and thanks.
For four days all was conference and delay,
But on the thirtieth, just at break of day,
The scouts reported that the foe was near.
There were a few small hillocks in the rear,
Forming a broken ridge that faced the west:
Upon the left, this naked ridge did rest
On a sharp spur of the Andes, that there jutted
Into the plain; and on the right abutted
On a thick wood, protecting that extreme:
Along the front ran a small boggy stream.
To this ground they retired, and there displayed
Their troops in order for the battle, led

By ALVAREZ, whose trade it was of old;
And there, like one determined, cool and bold,
He waited for the enemy.   BERNAL
Was placed upon the right, behind some small
And ragged cedars.   BLAS was on the left,
His cavalry withdrawn behind a drift
Of granite boulders, from the mountain rent.
The veteran GOMEZ, with his regiment,
And old BARBON with his, the centre held.
One half the men of ALVAREZ were placed
With BLAS, the other with BERNAL.   In haste
This being done, ALVAREZ took his post
Of leader, in the centre of the host.

They came like torrents swelling in the spring
Those brave and proven servants of the king;
In all the guady trappings of their trade,
Gay banners flying, bayonet and blade.
There was the Andalusian Regiment,
With dark green uniform; and near them went
Battalions from Galicia, and the brave
Biscayan cavalry; the old and grave
Artillery from Cordova;—troops, in fine;
From Spain's most eastern to her western line;
Their trumpets sounding an old Moorish tune.
Their leader, an old, gray-haired Catalun,
Who had learned tactics in Napoleon's school,
Threw out his heavy cavalry, to charge

The enemy's centre.   Dashing out they came,
Lances and sabres glittering like keen flame.
Charge upon charge they resolutely made,
But were repulsed.   Old Gomez, undismayed,
Stood stern as a rock, and poured his heavy fire
Into the squadrons with destruction dire.
And now the heavy infantry marched down,
And charged right on the centre.   Brightly shone
The gleaming bayonets, as, still and swift,
It came, the musketeers unbroken drift.
Gomez fell wounded, at the first fierce crash,
But still Barbon poured in his steady flash.
Bernal wheeled out, and charged in flank the foe,
And Blas poured down, and did upon them throw
His veteran cavalry, but all in vain.
Bernal was scattered; Blas attacked again,
And still again; and still he was repulsed.
Still the old Catalun urged on his men
Against the centre.   Alvarez had fought
Like a mad lion hemmed in his own den;
Provided all that his collected thought
Told him was needed; cheered his faltering troops;
Charged singly on the very thickest groups
Of the enemy; yet all in vain!   Still back
And back they pushed him; while his arm grew slack
With constant havoc, and his sight grew dim,
And by his side hung useless his left limb,
Struck by a sword whose owner struck no more.

Over red heaps, through puddles of dark gore,
The foe pressed onward. Hark! behind the hills
A single trumpet! At the echoing thrills
There was a pause; and sword and bayonet
Ceased their fierce work. Another trumpet yet!
And like the roar of a pine forest, came
A thousand horsemen. Many a heart grew tame
With doubt and fear. Not long was the delay,
For, as they came, like the hoarse thunders' bay
A thousand voices shouted "LIBERTAD!"
Blas and Bernal their shattered squadrons led
To either side, and down the horsemen came.
Alvarez knew that eye of flashing flame
That glittered in the front, and grew again
Strong as a lion maddened by sharp pain.
Two leaders came careering in the front,
Foremost to meet the battle's fiery brunt.
The one he knew: the other, who was he?
On the black squadrons came: that charge of dree
What troops could stand? Not those who there withstood
That coal-black steed was soon streaked o'er with blood:
Those serried riders rode down horse and man,
As trees are crushed before the hurricane.
In silence did they their fierce work of death,—
No shout, no cry, no wasting idle breath,—
But sudden wheel and fiery charge wherever
Their leader motioned,—he whose sabre never
Struck vainly in that fight,—whose arm ne'er slacked;

Whose course with dead and wounded wide was tracked.
Short was the contest: Alvarez once more
The shattered foe his bayonets drove before;
And Blas had gathered quickly in the rear
Of the black squadrons, and was charging near
Their silent captain; till, like foam and spray,
Melting before the tempest's wrath away,
The routed foe at all points fought no more,
But fled the field, in utter rout, before
The bloody tide of battle.

Valverde's day at last had come;
And every hot and hissing bomb,
That flew as if in savage glee,
Into the city of the sea,
Filled with fierce triumph his wild heart.
Shortly that proud and gorgeous mart,
The King's last stronghold in the land,
Was one wide wreck and ruin, and
They took it one bright day by storm.

Through the long, dreary solitudes
Of the wide streets all day there fell
The tramp of the stern sentinel,
Who kept his steady pace among

The broken rafters, and the throng
Of lifeless corpses; and thick smoke,
Which from the smouldering ruins broke,
O'er wounded men, whose piteous moans,
Rose from blood-dabbled pavement stones.
Valverde's victory was won,
And he had wreaked his will upon
The golden city, which had flung
Him out to starve and die among
The icy mountains.

Such, oh War!
Thy triumphs and thy trophies are!
Such are the things that earn men fame.
Oh, it should make Ambition tame,
Cause it to strew its starry crown
With dust and ashes; to sit down
And weep the triumphs it has won.
When will such curse be rained upon
This free and happy land of ours?
When will mad Tumult's thunder showers
Crush our proud cities to the ground?
When the wild cry of Plunder sound
Along our streets?—our dead be piled
Round burning shrines; our hands defiled
With the abomination of
A brother's gore? Oh, God of love!
Avert the day! Thou hast thus far

Warded from our bright natal star
The clouds of suicidal war.
Desert it not, good God! but let
It still in peaceful heavens be set
To shine upon our homes, and be
A beacon to the struggling free,
  Until the last great fight is won,—
Till kings no more fear Liberty,
  Nor men remember Washington.

––––––––––

Some days had passed. The city was at rest,
After the tumults that had torn its breast.
Carnage no more through street and palace hurried;
The ruins were removed, the dead were buried.
The living tide of busy human life
Again rolled on. Again the streets were rife
With splendor, wealth, pomp, beauty, as before.
The eagle flag was waving proudly o'er
Its domes and palaces; and here and there,
In the large squares stood the rude barracks, where
The soldiers quartered; and at every turn,
You met a sentinel, grim, silent, stern:
While now and then a sudden trumpet told
The city it was conquered.

From the cold
And snowy hills the golden sun had risen;
His ray rejoiced on dome and spire to glisten.
And danced into Antonia's chamber, through
The painted panes, taking therefrom a hue
Of soft, voluptuous, tender melancholy,
Such as we see within the dim and holy
Monotony of old cathedrals, where
The sanctity seems visible in the air;
Or in those fine old paintings, where you tell
At once the work of Titian or Raffaelle.

In her own room Antonia sate once more
In listless silence.   Her pale face still wore
The same sad look of utter desolation,
But there was something of stern elevation
And calm despair in her large, lustrous eyes,
A hopeless calm, that Fate's worst blows defies.
Her maiden dressed her for the bridal there,
And busied in the long, luxuriant hair
Her taper fingers, till she massed it round
A simple comb, and placed a rose or two
Amid the folds, whose white and creamy hue
Made the hair darker.   Then Antonia spoke:

"Give over, sweet Rosita!   'Tis enough!
Thy gentle hands, to-night, seem all too rough:
Perhaps it may have been my own poor head

That made me fancy pain. I go to wed
With one who heeds not looks, or else he had
But little judgment in selecting me,
So thin, so wan, so very pale and sad:
He careth not for beauty in a bride.
Nay? let it go so! He hath little pride,
And mighty love,—this future lord of mine.
It needeth not that dextrous art of thine;
When I am married, I shall get good looks,
And health and strength.   'Tis reading in sad books
Makes maidens thin."

                    "What books, my lady?"
                            "Those
Of the deep heart.   When wedded, I shall close
The pages up, and will again be well.
I have lost too much sleep of late.   The cell
To which I soon shall go hath sleep enough.
Nay, girl! I do not think thy hands are rough:
Weep not at that."

                    "Lady, it pains my heart
To see one, sweet and gentle as thou art,
So pale and thin, and using these sad words.
'Tis like the wild note of the anguished birds,
When their hearts break that they have lost their young."

"Weep on, then! I have wept, but long since flung
The last poor tear-drop from my heart; and now

I cannot weep. Weep on, Rosita! Thou
Art not a bride, or thou wouldst shed no tear.
Nay, thou wouldst laugh, as the glad hour drew near.
See! I can laugh, and do!"

       "Dear lady, change
The tenor of thy words! Thy looks are strange;
Thine eyes are brighter, too, than is their wont.
Ah! why do grief and sorrow ever hunt
The best and fairest?"

       "Hunted!—yes! 'tis so:—
By many wild-eyed hounds. Rosita know
I have had strange surmisings in my brain
About my reason; and at times I fain
Could wish for madness, that my utter woe
Might be forgotten in its frenzies. Oh!
Madness would be indeed a very heaven!
For then the sad and tortured heart might even
Moulder away, nor know its swift decline.
Perhaps in frenzy this poor brain of mine
Might entertain sweet dreams, and in them lose
The bitter memory of its many woes.
Oh! I could pray for madness!"

He said; and, with one mute obeisance more,
Passed from the Palace, towards the curving shore
Of the great sea turning his thoughtful course.

Night was upon the waters, and the hoarse
Voice of the ocean urged the unquiet winds
To dash upon her like vindictive fiends,
And rend her azure bosom.   Far in the west
Tempest and storm sat brooding on her breast;
Clouds lowered along the horizon's gloomy verge,
Like shadowy waves, cresting the thunder-surge,
And constantly the quick, unquiet tongue
Of lightning ran from crest to crest.   There rung
No voice of thunder.   The White gulls were out,
Wheeling in circles.   All betokened storm.

———————

Valverde stopped, and, gazing on the waste
Of the great sea, whose waves were shoreward cast,
And now boomed hollowly around his feet,
Uttered his thoughts aloud.

———————

What of Antonia, this momentous night?
The waning moon was some three hours high,
And struggled to unveil her ample eye
From the torn clouds.   Through a broad window fell,
At intervals, her gush of silver light
Into Antonia's chamber, through the bright
And varied staining of the gorgeous glass:

Borrowing from it, and from the heavy mass
Of damask curtains, more delicious hues,
And richer tints.   There did the maiden muse,
Seated upon the tesselated floor,
In the fickle moonlight.   As of one heart-sore,
Her wasted hands were crossed upon her breast,
Thin, and transparent as amethyst.
Her head hung drooping, like the heavy bud
Of a faint lily.   When the abundant flood
Of the rich moonlight fell upon her face
It met in her large eye a changeless gaze,
A ghastly paleness on her brow and cheek,
Which, plainer than all words could do, did speak
Utter despair.   Her glossy hair was wet,
And glittered in the moonlight like spun jet.
She had been wandering in the evening dew,
And her rich robes were with it dampened through;
For she had gone at moonrise to the spot
Where Ramon was to be, but found him not
She waited till she grew heart-sick and faint,
With disappointment, and then sadly bent
Her slow steps homeward.   There she sat, and filled
Her soul with strange conjectures, and with wild
And terrible thoughts of what had hindered him.
Then the suspicion, which, at first, a dim
And dreamy idea, undulated through
Her brain, returned, and soon and swiftly grew
Settled conviction;—she believed him gone

To his wild home the distant hill upon.
She shed no tear when this imagined truth
Came stunningly upon her. For sad youth
Seemed frail old age to her; and calm despair
Had dried the heart's springs; but she gasped for air,
Her aching eyes throbbed, but refused to shed
A single tear. Her bitter woes had led
Her soul to strange, dark, melancholy ways.
There was a slight, but still a palpable haze,
Of dull insanity upon her brain.
She shed no tear. Indeed, could one have looked
Into her heart, no single thought rebuked
Her lover for desertion. There she sate,
Utterly crushed, struck down by pitiless fate,
Too crushed for anger. Lightnings glittered through
The painted windows, and their lurid blue
Threw a death color on her pallid face.
The thunder-echoes that did wildly chase
Each other through the sky, smote on her ear
Unheeded, and her eyes closed not in fear,
But glittered in the lightning's blaze, and through
The utter darkness, with a fiery glow.

He left the priest at the great altar kneeling;
The organ through the lofty arches pealing,
The bridegroom, cleft to his chin upon the floor,
The father firmly held outside the door,

Raving as father never raved before.
On one strong arm his lovely mistress lay,
The other opened with his sword a way
Through the dead bridegroom's partisans, to where
His own dark riders in the open air
Waited his coming, ready for the march.

The black band left the City of the Sea,
With cheer, and shout, and joyful revelry,
For in the front their Captain slowly rode,
Towards the blue mountains, and their green abode;
And, blushing with delight, his lovely bride
Rode on a gentle palfrey by his side.
And well they understood their Captain's ear,
So occupied, their merriment could not hear,
Though loud and fast and furious it rung:
So, as they rode, this wild descant they sung:

ANDALUZ! ANDALUZ! *to the mountains!*
    Away from the toils of the plain,
To the pine-kings and rock-sheltered fountains,
    And our home of wild freedom again.
The eagle's free life we will follow once more,
And through fastness and valley for plunder we'll pour.

CATALUN! CATALUN! *sheathe the sabre!*
    Till the Captain calls for it again;—

Until then, for a life free from labor,
    From slavery, thraldom and pain.
We have given then freedom, and now 'tis but fair,
That we should be free, too, from trouble and care.

VISCAINO! VISCAINO! *a la frente!*
    The gray mountains soon will stream up;
Hurrah! for the rock-hold of plenty,
    And the bold rover's heaven, his cup!
Think not of the hills and green vales of Biscay,
With the wine's ruddy rain we'll wash that dream away.

CORDOVAN! CORDOVAN! *atiende!*
    Never turn up to heaven your eyes;
Our priest absolution shall lend you;
    Learn from him to be merry and wise
The city we leave cannot hope to compete
With the palace of rock that to-morrow we'll greet.

And where is the coward would falter,
    When summoned to follow his chief?
His neck shall be wed to the halter,
    He shall die the foul death of a thief.
We will risk every drop of our life's purple tide,
For Valverde the brave and his new-rescued bride.

                                              1836.

LES MARCHANDES.

FOR A FAIR.

PRINTEMPS.

SWEET SPRING stands blushing 'mid the flowers,
Heralded by benignant showers,
   And soft airs through the young leaves sighing
While winter flits to northern skies,
But scowls back as he ice-ward hies,
Enraged at her sweet sunny eyes,
As she with merry scorn defies
   The grim old graybeard flying:
Her lovely head with rosebuds crowned,
Her little feet that glad the ground,
While flitting by the lilied lakes,
And dancing rivulets, she makes
The earth its frosty fetters break,
And everything to life awake,
   As when the world began;
Such, but still merrier, lovelier yet,
My loving, mischievous, dear pet,
   My blue-eyed LILIAN.

AVRIL.

Young APRIL! waking of a sweet spring morn,
  When the fresh south-wind stirs the panting leaves;
And with loud welcome to the rose-lipped dawn,
  The mocking-bird floats heavenward from the eaves;—
Young April, laughing with her dark, bright eyes,
  Upon the timid flowers that scarce dare raise
Their jeweled foreheads toward the dewy skies,
  Lit by the crimson of the sun's first blaze:—
April, all smiles and blushes,—such and more,
Is our dear, little, timid ISADORE.

MAI.

The merry, laughing, rosy-fingered MAY!
  Whose snowy feet upon the thick grass tread,
As softly as the footsteps of young Day
  Upon a patient mountain's frosty head:
Young May, all smiles, with flowers thick-garlanded,
  And lips whose rich hue shames the envious rose,
  Cheeks like carnations blushing through spring-snows;
A graceful gait, a lovely leaf-crowned head;—
  Nor Spain nor Italy has ever seen
  A rarer maiden than young JOSEPHINE.

JUIN.

JUNE! with her lap wealthy with golden fruit;
   Young frolic June, under the green trees sleeping!
Her small head pillowed on a mossy root,
And on a snowy arm; one rosy foot,
   Half-hidden, through the enamored flowers is peeping;
The cool west-wind, with rapture almost mute,
   Sings a low tune; and gliding softly there,
The timid sunshine kisses her sweet face,
   And turns the thick cloud of her soft dark hair
Into a glory. Lo! she wakes, and grace
   And beauty breathe in every movement. Where,
In all the world, in what most fortunate place,
   Is face more lovely, eyes that brighter shine?
   Where shall we find a peer for CAROLINE?

LA MAITRESSE DE LA POSTE.

Let COLERIDGE sing his GENEVIEVE,
Who at his sad song could but grieve,
   And loved because she pitied;
And KEATS his lovely MADELINE,
With rosy mouth and eyes divine,
   And lips for kisses fitted;

That with her lover through the night,
Darkness without, within all light,
    To far-off countries flitted.
Let TENNYSON his LILIAN sing
    And lovely ORIANA,
And scale the skies with tireless wing,
    In praise of MARIANA,
I sing one lovelier by far,
One pure and gentle as a star,
    A modest, young, sweet creature,
In whose fair face a blushing grace
    Illumines every feature.
Pure as the stainless Alpine snows,
And lovelier than the sweet moss-rose,—
    What rhyme can, by what poet cannie,
Tell half the grace and beauty rare,
That fill like sunshine the glad air,
    And float round LITTLE ANNIE?

1850.

SONG.

Let the dreaming astronomer number each star,
  That at midnight peeps over its pillow of blue;
A pleasanter study to me is, by far,
  The orb that shines over a cheek's rosy hue.
Let the crazy astrologer search for his fates
  In the cusps and the nodes of his dim luminaries;
He is wiser, like me, who his fortune awaits,
  As told in the glance that in beauty's eye varies;
Who studies, as I do, the stars of the soul,
And cares not nor heeds how those over us roll.

I have studied them many a long summer eve,
  When the leaves and bright waters were quietly singing,
The science and learning that thence we receive,
  Is a joy and perfume to the memory clinging,
It is better than wasting the eyes and the brain,
  And youth's sunny season, intended for pleasure,
In delving for knowledge more useless and vain
  Than is to a squalid old miser his treasure.
I would give not one glimpse at the eyes that I love,
To know all the stars that are clustered above.

There was Lydia; no star was as bright as her eye,
    So soft, yet so proud, in its black, misty lashes;
While Harriet's, set in the clear summer sky,
    Would have shamed every orb in the azure that flashes;
There was Lizzy's, a gem 'neath her ivory brow,
    And Kate's, like Love's planet in still waters dreaming;
And Lilian, whose soul seems to shine on me now,
    As it shone of old time in her amber eyes beaming;
There was Mary, who kept me from conics and Greek,
While her eyes lit a love which the tongue could not speak.

There was Ann, whose dear smiles yet my visions inspire,
    And whose eyes bless my dreams like a light in the distance,
That over rude waters shoots welcoming fire,
    And to all good resolves and fair hopes lends assistance.
Let fate kindly light with such stars my dark way,
    For the few fleeting hours of my life-dream remaining;
I'll ask not for science to help me grow gray,
    I'll ask not for fame while my life-tide is waning;
I'll wish for no laurels, I'll ask for no prize,
But permission to study sweet lips and bright eyes.

                                                1833.

FRAGMENTS.

(OF AN UNFINISHED POEM.)

Dear woman! star of sad life's clouded heaven,
    I dedicate myself to thee again;
Fair woman! as man's guardian angel given,
    Thou to the soul art like the summer rain,
Or gentle dew that falls at morn or even;—
    Soother of woe, sweet comforter in pain;
Changing and beautiful like the sunset's hue,—
I dedicate myself again to you.

Myself, my pen, my heart, my hand,—yea, all,
    All that I have or am, though valueless;
Despise it not, although the gift be small!
    I swear my homage by the mystic tress,
The showers of light from radiant eyes that fall,
    And soothe sick hearts in their sad loneliness;
By everything ethereal and human,
Which goes to constitute a perfect woman.

Man fell for thee, dear woman! it is said,—
    And in thy arms it seemed to him but slight,
His loss of Heaven. For thee, too, he has bled,
    And sunken cheerfully in death's long sleep;
For thee he has from fame and honor fled,
    And counted shame, disgrace and pain but light,
While pressing thee to his enraptured breast,
And with the wealth of thy sweet kisses blest.

Thou hast inspired the poet's sweetest songs:

    And he who has not loved before thy shrine,
Glowed in thy love, and angered at thy wrongs,

    Is no liege-man of poetry divine.
To thee the warrior's scimitar belongs,

    And leaps like lightning when the cause is thine;
And thou hast kingdoms, empires overthrown,
By the strong magic that is all thine own.

Thou art the soother of the sad man's dreams;

    Thy spirit comes to him when night is still,
Pressing soft fingers, like ethereal beams

    Of sunshine on his brow of pain, until
Under her influence again he deems

    That he is happy, and glad tears distil
Away the sadness of his wasted soul;
And when the day-floods on his eyelids roll,

The memory of the vision still is sweet,

    Making his sorrows more benign and calm.
Thou to the weary traveller's aching feet

    Givest new strength, when, with expanded palm,
Sweet Fancy comes, and woman seems to greet;

    And then, unmoved, he hears the thunder-psalm,
And the stern wind's storm-gathering lament,
The roar of Nature's mighty armament.

So hast thou been to me, when I have stood
    On many a mountain's bald and snowy peak,
In the clear ether's silent solitude,
    Whereon the storms their sharpest anger wreak,—
On cliffs of ice that there for ages brood,
    Feeding clear streams that far below outbreak.
There dreams of thee have lit the darkling mind,
And cheered the heart before so sad and blind.

When I have stood my long and weary guard,
    Upon the illimitable western plain,
While round me the harsh wind blew sharp and hard,
    And not a star shone through the misty mane
Of the cold clouds that toward the thunder-scarred
    Old mountains hurried, big with hail and rain:
I saw in visions those dear amber eyes,
To gain whose love, life were small sacrifice.

And since I ceased my houseless wandering,
    Once more to live and toil amid mankind,
Still to the memory of those eyes I cling,
    Lost to whose light, I should be truly blind.
And thou, dear woman, art the only thing,
    That nerves the heart, and braces up the mind,
To struggle bravely with the selfish world,
Like a lone boat amid the breakers hurled.

For far off in the aisles of memory,
    I see the faces that I bowed before,
While wandering on the shore of life's blue sea,
    And playing with its waves:—those loved of yore:
And still they have dominion over me,
    And day by day I worship them the more,—
The loved, the lost, the beautiful, and bright,
Whose radiant eyes would make mid-noon of night.

Ah, ye were made to lure mankind from sin,
    And lead to heaven,—ye blessed and beautiful!
And could one leave the great world's busy din,
    The selfish, the ill-natured, and the dull,
Finding a heaven your loving arms within,
    Life were all bliss: it were indeed to cull
Sweet flowers, rare fruits, unwounded by the thorn,
And make of life one long and lovely morn.

Woman is ever loved most, most adored,
    When gentle, trusting and affectionate:
Then avariciously her love we hoard
    As a miser's gold: we scoff at scowling Fate;
And like an argosy that has on board
    Of spices and rare silks a mighty freight,
We spread top-gallant sails, and plough the sea,
With confident keel, the fair winds blowing free.

And yet we love an under-current of pride,

    A flash of fire in the softest, bluest eye,
As even the quietest river's placid tide

    Will flash with foam when rocks beneath it lie!
For this the loveliest have been deified,

    And men to gain a smile been glad to die:
And these, in times of Knighthood and Romance,
Oft set in rest the warrior's trusty lance.

Often she's like some fragrant, thankless flower,

    That fed by the blushing dawn with honey-dew,
Gives her whole heart to the sun, at day's first hour,

    But when he shines most constant and most true,
And rains upon her an abundant shower

    Of light that is his love and being too,
Then closes her cold heart and turns away,
Ungrateful from the enamored god of day.

"Once more upon the ocean, yet once more,"

    Launched in my frail bark of unstudied rhyme;
Upon that deep along whose sandy shore

    Are strewed bright hopes, gay visions, schemes sublime,
Brilliant imaginings from fancy's store,

    Wild aspirations, follies, ghastly crimes:—
On this rough ocean I unfurl my sail,
And bend my cheek to feel the rising gale.

Here by a high and beaked promontory,

    Its name, Neglect, lie many a youngster, dead;

Some whose great griefs are told in piteous story,

    And some that ever from men's knowledge fled,

Toiled in still cells and solitudes for glory,

    With a miser's care night's long hours husbanded,

And startled the dull world with wondrous songs,

Filled with the sad tale of their many wrongs;

Until their life faded and paled away,

    Like one low wail of a long agony;

Or fever-fire turning their dark hair gray,

    Burned the tense brain into insanity,

Gloomy as night.   For these, alas! are they

    That were the servitors of Poetry;

Unfit to embark in the mad world's furious strife,

They sank beneath the howling storms of life.

Here they all lie, as if almost alive,

    With deep, dark eyes, like lamps, that in the night,

Within a deep recess for mastery strive

    With insolent darkness.   Through the forehead's white,

Veins blue as seas wherein pearl-fishers dive

    Yet swell transparent in the garish light;

While, as if life's long struggle were just o'er,

Nostril and lips are slightly stained with gore.

And these are they whose songs are now the food
    And inspiration of ten thousand souls;
And while this sea, in its great solitude,
    Laves their white feet, and, never quiet, rolls
The sad monotony of its blue flood,
    On their dead ears, they live in immortal scrolls,—
BYRON and SHELLEY, CHATTERTON and KEATS,
SAVAGE, and all their co-unfortunates.

On this great sea I dare to steer my bark,
    Sleep in its calm, nor tremble at its storm,
Dart through its mist and lightnings like the lark,
    And sing like him when the bright sun shines warm;
Ride its wild swells, to its hoarse breakers hark;—
    For the great waves that crush the frigate's form,
Spare the small skiffs that over shallows glide,
And where the tall ship sinks, they safely ride.

Fame! Thou bright beacon set amid the shoals,
    Where, like the wrecker's light, thou lurest on,
The mariner to death!—Thou, to the souls
    Of poets and philosophers the sun,
By whose clear beams they write their golden scrolls,
    Drinking deep draughts at fabled Helicon;—
It were the falsest of all things, to say
That thou hast lured *me* not along my way.

For thee young poets from the world's vortex go,

    To dry their hearts up by the midnight lamp;

For thee the chemist labors, sure and slow,

    Sounding great nature's secrets: thou dost stamp,

And armies all the wide world overflow,

    Scale the grim breach, defend the desperate camp:

Thou dost inspire the eloquent orator,

And senates, nations quake his voice before.

And yet thine empire is not absolute;—

    The love of gold and woman share with thee

The human heart, and thy control dispute.

    The latter thou o'ercomest frequently;

Thy fiery voice prevails against the mute

    And gentle eloquence of woman's plea;

Enticed by thee the soldier leaves his bride,

Hoping to be by glory deified.

Lo! the white shadow of my venturous sail

    Flits over thy waves.   Fortune perhaps may fill

My canvas with a favorable gale,

    And so atone for all my want of skill.

If not, I shall not be the first to fail,

    And, baffled often, I will struggle still:

Open my heart when death has stiffened it,

And in its deepest core you'll find "Fame" writ!

Down with those stars and stripes that flout the sky!
    Off with that banner from the indignant deep!
Chain up your eagle from his flight on high
    Bid him no more over the ocean sweep,
Scream to the wind, turn to the sun his eye!
    Down, down with Freedom from each rampart steep,
And promontory tall, and prairie wide,
Where she hath been, till now, so deified!

Listen! how Europe rings from end to end
    With scoff and jeer, and hatred's bitter scorn!—
Her Kings sit smiling at the clouds that bend,
    Threatening wild storm, over a land now torn
With mad dissension; ready all to lend
    Their hosts, still more to darken our bright morn,
And aid in this unhallowed, wretched strife,
So lately sprung of treason into life.

Think, think, dear brothers, of our days of glory,
    The splendid memories that cluster round
The names of those ancestral patriots hoary,
    Who fought to gain all that ye would confound:
Read of their great deeds the surpassing story,
    And turn again, before the awful sound
Of shame's dark ocean stun the startled soul,
And over you its raging surges roll!

Follow no longer where those madly lead

    Whom crazed ambition and blind rage have brought

To do this traitorous work, this wicked deed!

    Turn back! Along the path you tread is nought

But shame, disgrace and ruin! Ye will bleed,

    Not like those heroes who in old time fought

And nobly bled in their dear country's cause:

Ye war against that country and her laws.

Look on the future with prophetic eye!

    See on your green plains armies gathering,

As mists collect when a great storm is nigh!—

    Mighty storm!—Along the hill-slopes cling

The light-horse, like dark flocks of birds, that fly

    Before the wind with rapid, restless wing.

Here move the rifles, orderly and swift,

And there the musketeers' unbroken drift.

The battle!—Listen to the musketry!

    While ever and anon amid its roll,

Roars the loud cannon: now the cavalry

    Dash down, like waves against a rocky mole,

Built strong and far in the bosom of the sea.

    The stern battalions charge as with one soul;

And now, like waves breaking in spray and rain,

The shattered ranks go floating back again.

The fight is over: misery scarce begun!

    Count, if you can, the multitude of slain;

The hoary head lies glittering in the sun,

    Pillowed upon the charger's misty mane;

And here, with hair like delicate moonlight spun,

    A boy lies dying, with the crimson stain

Around his nostril and upon his lips;

While just below his heart the red rain drips.

The banner of your state in the dust lies low,

    Rebellion draws to an untimely end;

Fair girls amid the horrid carnage go,

    And anxiously above the corpses bend,

Seeking among your dead or those of the foe,

    A father or a brother, or dear friend;

And constantly upon the tortured air

Rings the loud wail of agonized despair.

Where are your leaders, they who madly led

    Your feet to this deep perilous abyss?

There lie the best and noblest, with the dead,

    Happy in their entire unconsciousness;

The noisiest, like cowards, far have fled,

    Pursued by scorn's indignant, general hiss,

To distant lands, that liberty disowns,

And crouch there in the shadows of old thrones.

Is this indeed to be your wretched fate?
    Disgraced, degraded, humbled, and abased,
Fallen, forever from your high estate,
    To wander over Tyranny's dark waste,
Crouch like scared slaves around a despots' gate,
    Bend at his nod, at his stern mandate haste?—
Oh, Thou, who once Thy favor to us lent,
Avert the doom, Father Omnipotent!

Turn then! before the final seal is set
    To your apostasy!—before the flood
Waked by your madness, which it bears as yet,
    Shall overwhelm you with a sea of blood!
Turn back! before your lovely land is wet
    With crimson spray;—while treason's in its bud;—
Before the avenging angel spreads his wing,
Where whose dark shadow falls no grass will spring.

Turn! that whenever men have made your grave,
    They say not, as they pile the parting sod,
"Here lies a traitor," or, "Here rots a slave."
    Turn! lest old men some day above it nod,
And warn their boy to be no traitorous knave,
    But reverence his country and his God,
Lest he deserve a doom as sad as yours,
The world's stern sentence, that like time endures.

Have ye been never troubled in your dreams,
    With spirits, rising from your fathers' tombs,
And in the darkness, or the moon's thin gleams,
    Warning you of those miserable dooms,
Which hunt the traitor to the world's extremes,
    As wolves hunt men, far in Siberian glooms?
Ah! these must haunt you,— these most noble ones,
These heroes, Liberty's illustrious sons.

Had I a sire who thus from the grave could rise,
    Point to his wounds, and say, "With these I bought
That freedom which you madly now despise,
    And sealed the compact that your hands have sought
To break and shatter,"—I would close mine eyes,
    For shame that I to sin had so been wrought,
And heap up dust and ashes on my head,
For knave corrupt, or idiot misled.

There is an isle, circled by southern seas,
    Far in a soft clime of perpetual spring,
Where the voluptuous odor-laden breeze,
    Is never chilled in its far wandering
By churlish frost; no winters ever free
    The delicate flowers, or numb the bee's thin wing,
As in this harsh, inhospitable clime,
Where we, unfortunate, do waste our time.

And all along its shores are sunny beaches,
    Paved smoothly with the golden, jewelled sand;
And deep among mossed rocks are narrow reaches,
    Where the lost waves frolic along the strand.
On every side the broad blue ocean stretches,
    Gemmed with no island, rimmed with no green land:
This diamond of the sea shines there alone,
The only jewel of that distant zone.

Within the isle are clustered great broad trees,
    With fruits and flowers, young buds and nested birds,
Fed by delicious winds from calm, far seas,
    With honey-dew.   Like a fond lover's words,
Or music's most voluptuous harmonies,
    These winds float here and there in whispering herds,
Their light wings heavy with rich odors, where
Sedate bees ride, and their rich freightage bear.

Back from the shore the mountains overlook
    The island and the broad realm of the sea,
Haughty and high.   The upper element shook
    His thick snows there, when time began to be,
And there, to the curious sun a close-sealed book,
    It coldly glitters.   Sleeping silently
Below, great trees robe the rude mountain-side,
Through whose high tops the white clouds flocking ride.

And light and love ever inhabit here.

Within this beautiful and happy isle:
Through the green woods wander the dappled deer,

And feeds the snowy antelope; and while
Round the great trunks the frightened shadows peer,

That bless the grass, and make the flowers to smile,
With its great lamping eyes the shy gazelle
Looks out from every nook and ivied dell.

The simple people in that paradise

Live as men lived when the young world was green,
In primitive innocence supremely wise;

Rich with content.   No prisons there are seen,
No palaces offend plebian eyes,

Their simple laws say ever what they mean;
And happy under patriarchal sway,
They see glad hours and calm days glide away.

One of these islanders, some years ago,

Seeking for pearls and rosy, wrinkled shells,
To deck his sweetheart's hair, took heart to row,

By fair skies tempted, into the outer swells,
Beyond the coral-shoals, his light canoe;

And diving there into the sea's deep wells,
Gathered white pearls and crimson coral-stems,
And blushing shells,—old ocean's favorite gems.

"And then God's organ pealed its thunder-psalm,
And the whole sea seemed with one groan to lift
Into white foam, thick as an Alpine drift."

He noted not that one small, grayish cloud,
　　Low in the west, the swift storm's harbinger,
Spread swiftly upward, like an unrolling shroud,
　　Dark as its native midnight sepulchre:
That armies of wild winds did skyward crowd,
　　Like shadowy cohorts riding with mad spur,
Scourging the cloud-surge, that in great waves piled,
Grew every moment more sublimely wild.

He hurried towards the circling coral-reef,
　　Urging his frail skiff on, with wild alarm;
But the storm stooped: there was a very brief
　　And terrible stillness, a portentous calm,
Like stunned despair, or sudden, speechless grief,
　　And then God's organ pealed its thunder-psalm,
And the whole sea seemed with one groan to lift
Into white foam, thick as an Alpine drift.

Then the gale smote him: seas of spray drove by;
　　But not a wave could lift its struggling head
Into the air.　From the black, boiling sky,
　　Thick torrents poured like rivers filled and fed
With great spring-rains; sharp hail shot hissing by.
　　And with incessant blaze, around his head,
Flashed the white lightning, while the awful voice
Of thunder bade the hurricane rejoice.

And seaward sped the light, thin, frail canoe,

    While he clung to it with a mute despair;

Long trained the ocean's realms to wander through,

    His skiff capsized, he rose again to the air,

And still held fast, still onward with it flew:

    And still the storm-god, from his western lair,

Urged on his slave, the furious hurricane,

Till night fell, when he called him home again.

And then the clouds began to break and part,

    And soon shone out the broad, bright, patient moon,

But still the winds shrieked, and the sea's great heart

    Swelled in vast waves. Lightnings, retreating soon,

Lingered upon the horizon yet, to dart

    Their Parthian arrows; then came night's high noon,

And all the stars shone, trembling at the roar

Of winds and waves that smote the sky's blue floor,

Righting his skiff, till morning he outrode

    The dying wind, and eastward still fled on;

And when above the orient barrier strode,

    In all his summer pomp, the regal sun,

And while he journeyed on his westering road,

    Till evening came when the long day was done,

Still it sailed there, that light and fragile thing,

Like the faint hopes that to a sad heart cling.

And all that night, thinking of home he lay,
　　For the ocean, like a stunned hope, now was still:
On the sea's verge he seemed to see the spray
　　Break over his loved coral-reefs,—the hill
That cast its shadow on his home,—the gray
　　And mist-crowned mountain,—the clear, dancing rill,
That fed his flowers,—the trees that over the eaves
Of his small cottage shook their sheltering leaves.

At dawn he slept, slept soundly, nor awoke,
　　Till noon was shining brightly on his eyes;
And still around no living object broke
　　The broad monotony of sea and skies.—
Yes!—scarce distinguished from the flickering smoke
　　Of the sun's heat, a something he descries:
Hope gleams once more, a feeble, fitful spark,
And once again he urges on his bark.

On the horizon soon the object grows
　　To a gallant ship, full-rigged,—ah, joyful sight!—
That while the fair breeze on her quarter blows,
　　Over the waters wings her steady flight,
Startling the sleepy monsters that repose
　　Deep in the sea: shaking her canvas white,
Near him she slides;—her sails are thrown aback,
She halts, as halts a racer on the track,

Tossing his mane back on the eager wind:

    They cast a rope; the stranger gains the deck;
Tottering and weak, with hunger faint and blind.

    Then spurning from her side the skiff's frail wreck,
Onward she leaps, while on the deck reclined,

    But little does the stranger know or reek
Whither they bear him, so he be with men,
And not cast forth upon the waves again.

A month or two they cruised about those seas,

    Touching at many a green and flowery isle,
Where patient insects had by slow degrees

    Done giants' work, and builded many a pile
Of rock and reef; then with a favoring breeze,

    Homeward they turned, and voyaged many a mile,
And bent around the Southern Giant's Horn,
That Cape of dread to mariners forlorn.

And so they northward sailed, until there grew

    Cold on the iron visage of the sea;
Sharp hail fell thick, stinging their garments through,

    Ice gathered on the cordage silently,
And then hove up the shores, long, low, and blue,

    And one great promontory on the lee,
Where stood the homes of many in the ship.
Then quivered many a firm and manly lip.

And out of many a stern and fearless eye,
  Warm tears fell, on the weather-bronzed cheek.
How the heart softens when its home is nigh!
  The iron nerves, like children's become weak!
Oh, that I too might feel before I die
  This blessed joy!   If love again could speak
One word of gentle greeting in my ear,
How bright and sunny would the world appear!

1833.

LINES.

(IN ONE MONTH I SHALL BE IN THE PRAIRIE, AND UNDER THE MOUNTAINS IN ANOTHER.)

Once more unto the desert! who
    Would live a slave, when he can free
His heart from thraldom thus? O who?
       Slave let him be.

Once more unto the desert! now
    The world's hard bonds have grown too hard.
No more, oh heart! in dungeons bow,
       And caves unstarred.

Heart! bid the world farewell: thy task
    Is done;—perhaps thy words may live;—
Thou hast no favor now to ask,
       And few to give.

Thou has writ down thy thoughts of fire,
    And deep communion with thine own
Sad spirit; now thy broken lyre
       Makes its last moan.

Thou hast laid out thy secrecy
        Before the world, and traced each wave
Of feeling, from thy troubled sea
                Unto its cave.

Within thy dim recesses, where
        The feelings most intense are hidden;
Thou hast outborne thence to the air
                Thy thoughts, unbidden.

And now unto the desert!   Why
        Am I to be a slave forever?
To stay amid mankind, and die
                Like a scorched river,

Wasting in burning sands away?
        Am I to toil, and watch my heart
And spirit, hour by hour decay,
                Still not depart?—

                        .

To pour the treasure of my soul
        Upon the world's parched wilderness,
And feel no answering echo roll
                My ear to bless?

Once more unto the desert!   There
    I ask nor wealth, nor hope, nor praise,
Nor gentle ease, nor want of care
        On my dark ways;

Nor fame, nor friends, nor joy, nor leisure—
    Here I must have them all, or die,
Or lead a life devoid of pleasure—
        Such now lead I.

No life of pain and toil for me!
    Of home unhoped for—friends unkind!
Better the desert's waveless sea,
        And stormy wind.

Better a life amid the wild
    Storm-hearted children of the plain,
Than this, with heart and soul defiled
        By sorrow's rain.

Out to the desert! from this mart
    Of bloodless cheeks, and lightless eyes,
And broken hopes, and shattered hearts,
        And miseries.

Out to the desert! from the sway
  Of falsehood, crime, and heartlessness;
Better a free life for a day
    Than years like this.

Once more unto the desert, where
  My gun and steed shall be my friend:
And I shall ask no aidance there—
    As little lend.

Farewell, my father-land! Afar
  I make my last and kind farewell.
I did think to have seen thee—ah!
    How hopes will swell!

Farewell, forever! Take the last
  Sad gift, my father-land, of one
Struck by misfortune's chilling blast,
    Yet still thy son.

Farewell, my land! Farewell, my pen!
  Farewell, hard world—thy harder life!
Now to the desert once again!
    The gun and knife!

Arkansas Territory, May 25, 1833.

JANE.

She is not beautiful, but in her eyes
  No common spirit manifests itself,
So mild, so gentle, so serenely wise,
  Yet gay as that of any dainty elf,
That dances on green turf, by starlit skies;
  And such a friend is she, so firm and true,
So free from envy, malice, prejudice,
  And constant as the sky's unchanging blue:
She shines like some most lustrous, lovely star,
  Which men adore because it dazzles not;—
And though I waste away my life afar,
  Yet in this mountainous and savage spot,
I think of her as one who soothed my care,
  And did her best to keep me from despair.

1832.

AGAPOU PNEUMA.

Thou must have altered in the two long years
Which thou hast passed since I beheld thee, Ann!
For then thou was just budding into life,
And Hopes, with fiery eyes, thy heart did fan,
And gray Grief's tears
Had not assailed thee.   Thou wast very rife
With budding beauty, which is now full blown
In all the sunny spring of womanhood.
Thy spirit shone
Like an ethereal angel's in thy face:
There was a proud and an impassioned tone
Within thy voice, that breathed from off the soul
A strong enchantment on a heart like mine.
Thou wast a glorious being in thy bud;
But in thy blossoms, thou must be divine.
Oh! I can fancy thee in all thy power,
In all thy beauty and magnificence;
Thine eyes so beautiful and so intense,
Raining into the heart their starry shower;
Thy raven hair shining above a brow
Replete with Italy and with divinity;
Thy form so slight, so very delicate,
Yet swelling proudly with thy uncontrolled

And uncontrollable spirit. Oh! how cold
Seems beauty to me, when I think on thee,
Thou beautiful and bright and fiery star!
And I afar
Bow down before thee, though I have no hope
To win or wear thee near my withered heart.

Thou wast too full of uncontrolled romance,
Too full of Poetry's impassioned trance,
Too full of soul, to live amid the world.
Thy body to thy soul was like a cloud,
In which the silver arrows of the sun
Stay not, but pass wherever they are hurled;
'Twas like the clear transparent element,
That shows the emerald beneath it pent,
Nor robs one ray. Thy soul breathed in thy face,
And lay upon it like a visible mist.
Thou wast not fit for life's realities;
The world all seemed too fair unto thine eyes;
Thou wast too full of hope, and faith, and trust—
And art, perhaps, ere this, most undeceived.
Thy heavenly eyes, perhaps, have been, and are
Dim with the dew which wastes away the heart—
And such a heart! Oh! it is sad to think
That all the richer feelings of the soul
Are but its torment; that the lustrous star
Which shines the brightest, soonest wastes away;
Yea—that the gifted soul, that will, must drink

Of poetry, romance, and glowing love,
Kindles a fire that must consume itself!
And thou wilt be unhappy.   Never one
Was gifted with thy fervid, trusting soul,
And went through life unscathed and sorrowless.
And thou and I, too, soon will reach our goal.
The world, which ought thy glorious spirit bless,
Will chill thee, Ann! and make thy heart grow cold;
And thou wilt never, save in grief, be old.
This, this it is, which makes me love thee.   I
Feel that there is between my soul and thine
A sympathy of feeling and of fate,
Which binds me to thee with a deathless tie,
Time has already seen *my* heart decay,
Where death has trod.   Yet, though it waste away,
Daily and nightly, still the core is left,
And burns for thee with all its former fire;
There is concentered all.

                    I would to God
Thou couldst be mine, Ann! for the few short years
Left me to live; that when my death was nigh,
Thou mightest be near me with thy glorious eyes,
Shining like stars into my waning soul—
Thy arms be wreathed around my neck—thy lip
Pressed to my throbbing brow—thy voice
Hushing Despair and that unconquered fiend,
Ambition—till it were

No pain to die, and breathe upon the wind
My last low gasp.   Methinks if thou wast mine,
I might forget the world, and wo, and care,
And let them wreak their worst on me: perhaps,
My heart might be too strong for them to crush:
It may not be.
My fate is fixed.   I ask the world a boon,
I cannot, will not, Ann, demand of thee:
Henceforth I pray the world that it forget
That I have lived.

                  All that I now have left,
Is death and my own wo; and I will die,
Unknown, unnamed.   The world shall not be nigh,
To mark the quivering lip—the stopping heart—
The closing eye—the fingers clenched in death—
The last low moan, when with the parting shiver,
I murmur *Ann.*

                  Arkansas Territory, 10th March, 1832.

TO ANN.

These lines are to thee; and they come from a heart,
Which hath never to thee spoken aught but the truth,
And which fain would, ere life from its fountains depart,
Speak to thee of the sorrows which clouded its youth.

And think not 'tis only to show a fair rhyme,
Or a glittering thought to the eyes of the world;
Oh no! 'tis a motive more purely sublime;
My wings of ambition forever are furled.

'Tis my love, my devotion, which *will* find a tongue,
And utter its thoughts before life and I sever;
'Tis the heart which was bruised, and then wantonly flung
On the shore of life's sea, to be trampled forever.

For its words, and its thoughts, and its feelings have been
Miconceived, misconstrued and traduced for long years;
And 'twould fain, from the general calumny, win
One heart, that might water its grave-sod with tears.

For the world, I defy it and dare it; it hath
No power, no terror, no lash, over me;
I ask not the light of its smile in my path,
And its pity or frown might as well urge the sea.

I owe it, and ask it no favor; full well
I have proven its friendship, its mercy, its love;
But thou hast upon me a charm and a spell,
That through life and in death will be able to move.

I would show that the heart which the world hath reviled,
Whose passions have been like the waves of the sea,
Whate'er it hath been—how ungoverned and wild—
Hath been constantly true in devotion to thee.

That devotion to thee, love, hath never been told:
Perhaps 'twas unnoticed; the feeling most deep
Has the semblance of something unfeeling and cold;
The grief most o'erwhelming but seldom can weep.

And readier tongues spake their tale in thine ear,
And told thee their love with full many a sigh;
Perhaps thou wast dazzled by that and the tear,
And read not my love in the heart and the eye.

I told not my love—it were cruel to ask
One like thee, with misfortune and sorrow to wed,
To wear away life as an incessant task,
And pillow on Poverty's bosom thy head—

Till I turned from the green and the delicate lanes
Of home, love and joy, which were darkened with gloom,
And shivered, unflinching, the multiplied chains,
Which are woven round all when the heart is in bloom.

Since then, day by day, my lone heart hath decayed,
With a slow, but a certain, and deadly decline;
O'er its waste and its wilderness riseth no blade,
Which may say with its greenness—"Wo! all is not thine."

And though I must die ere my deity sphere
Be revealed from the storm which holds heaven at will,
I *must* turn to the place where it ought to appear,
And worship its light till my pulses be still.

It may be that I am to live till my cup
Of affliction be filled and o'erflow at the brim;
Till the mist and the blood from the heart shall rise up,
When its last hope is gone—its last vision is dim;

Till thou hast become, in thy beauty, the bride
Of some other less wild, and less passionate lover;
Then the beacon is merged in the hungering tide—
Then the heart hath been crushed, and its struggle is over.

Arkansas Territory, February, 12, 1833.

"ΕΠΟΣ.

CHAUNTED BY JACK SAVAGE, AT THE LIFE-WAKE OF THE FINE ARKANSAS
GENTLEMAN, WHO DIED BEFORE HIS TIME, 1859.*

A gentleman from ARKANSAS, not long ago, 'tis said,

Waked up one pleasant morning, and discovered he was
dead;

He was on his way to Washington, not seeking for the
Spoils,

But rejoicing in the promise of a spree at JOHNNY COYLE'S.

>One spree at Johnny Coyle's, one spree at Johnny
>Coyle's;
>And who would not be glad to join a spree at
>Johnny Coyle's?

He waked and found himself aboard a rickety old boat;

Says the ferryman, when questioned, "on the Styx you are
afloat;"

"What dead?" said he;—"indeed you are," the grim old
churl replied;

"Why, then, I'll miss the spree at Coyle's," the gentle-
man replied.

>One spree at Johnny Coyle's, &c.

---

*Occasioned by a report that Gen. Pike had died a month previously.

Old Charon ferried him across the dirty, sluggish tide,

But he swore he would not tarry long upon the further side;

The ancient ghosts came flocking round upon the Stygian shore;—

"But," said he, "excuse me; I must have at Coyle's one frolic more."

One spree at Johnny Coyle's, &c.

Horace and old Anacreon in vain would have him stay;

From all those ancient fogies he made haste to get away;

For his Majesty, King Pluto, he was bound at once to see,

And at Johnny Coyle's, on Friday night, alive or dead to be.

One spree at Johnny Coyle's, &c.

Old Cerberus growled savagely, as he approached the gate;

"But," said he, "I've seen too many dogs for you to make me wait;

"If you show your teeth at me, my dog, your windpipe I shall twist;

"For if I were not to be at Coyle's, I'm sure I should be missed."

One spree at Johnny Coyle's, &c.

He crossed the adamantine halls, and reached the ebon
throne,

Where gloomy Pluto frowned, and where his queen's soft
beauty shone.

"What want you here?" the Monarch said: "Your
Majesty," said he,

"Permission at one frolic more at Johnny Coyle's to be."

One spree at Johnny Coyle's, &c.

"As Orpheus came, and yet returned, to breathe the upper
air,

"So I your royal bounty crave, once more to venture there;

"Give me one night—no more;—Alas! SUCH nights are
all too few!

"One more refection of the Gods; and then, good world,
adieu!"

One spree at Johnny Coyle's, &c.

" 'Tis not for power, or wealth, or fame, I hanker to
return,

"Nor that love's kisses once again upon my lips may burn;

"Let me but once more meet the friends that long have
been so dear,

"And who, if I'm not there, will say, 'Would God that he
were here!' "

One spree at Johnny Coyle's, &c.

"Are you not dead?" the King then said. "Well, what
of that?" said he,

"If I AM dead, I've not been WAKED, and buried decently."

"And why," the Monarch cried, "desire again to share
life's toils,

"For the sake of one good frolic more, even at Johnny
Coyle's?"

One spree at Johnny Coyle's, &c.

"We've Nectar and Ambrosia here; we do not starve
the dead."—

"Did you ever sample canvas-backs and terrapins?" he said:

"The table of your Majesty well served is, I dare say;

"But I wish you were at Johnny Coyle's, to taste
his St. Peray."

One spree at Johnny Coyle's, &c.

"If its good company you want," the King said, "We've
the best—

"Philosophers, Poets, Orators, Wits, Statesmen, and the
rest;

"The courtiers of the good old times, the gentlemen most
rare."—

Says he, "With those I'll meet at Coyle's your folks will
not compare."

One spree at Johnny Coyle's, &c.

Says the King, "There's Homer here, and all the bards of
 p   ancient Greece,

"And the chaps that sailed away so far to fetch the golden
fleece;

"We've Tully, Horace, and Montaigne." Says he, "I'll
match the lot,

"If you'll let me go to Johnny Coyle's, and fetch them
on the spot."

One spree at Johnny Coyle's, &c.

"Whom will you bring?" said Pluto.—"CHARLEY BOTELER
first I'll bring,

Facile princeps of good fellows, always ready for a ring,

In whose presence Alcibiades eclipsed shall hide his head,

And Charley shall take rank among the Past's illustrious
dead."

One spree at Johnny Coyle's, &c.

"The next shall WALTER LENOX be, the generous and true,

Who loves the old friends better than he e'er can love the
new;

JACK SAVAGE next, who, heart in hand, demands who wants
a friend?

Where Freedom is to fight for, where the Right is to defend?

One spree at Johnny Coyle's, &c.

"I'll bring you BURWELL, Prince of Wits and Prince of
Statesmen, too,

Who like Bayard, the dauntless Knight, reproach and fear
ne'er knew;

ASH. WHITE, whose heart, defying time, is always in its
youth;

GEORGE GIDEON, grand in honesty, grand in the simple
truth.

One spree at Johnny Coyle's, &c.

"I'll bring you PHILIP BARTON KEY, the Roman Tully's
peer.

And JONAH HOOVER, frank and brave, straight-forward
and sincere;

McGUIRE, the generous, liberal friend, the patron of the
arts,

Who, not content with fortune, takes delight in winning
hearts.

One spree at Johnny Coyle's, &c.

"Modest, reserved and silent, ingenuous, bashful, shy,

SHELTON MCKENZIE shall descend, your drinkables to try;

The generous boon-companion he, the genial humorist,

Who counts his friends by thousands, and ne'er drops one
from the list.

One spree at Johnny Coyle's, &c.

"And ALEXANDER DIMITRY'S great soul shall come to claim
Its place among the giants, and upon the roll of fame;
The noble by God's patent he, the fiery and the frank,
Who at the living springs of Truth its inspiration drank.

One spree at Johnny Coyle's, &c.

"I'll bring the Empresario, BEV. TUCKER, who shall win
From Pericles Aspasia, if he chooses to go in;
The man without an enemy, the wit, the Sheridan
In whom two continents confess the gallant gentleman.

One spree at Johnny Coyle's, &c.

"The Barrow-Knight, BEN PERLEY POORE, shall come queer
   tales to tell,
Who as writer, friend, wit, gentleman, all he aims to do,
   does well;
GEORGE FRENCH, our paragon, shall come, to charm your
   ghosts with song,
Till Tartarus seems Elysium, to the fascinated throng.

One spree at Johnny Coyle's, &c.

"HUGH CAPERTON shall come likewise, the generous
  Advocate,
Who never lets the Right upon Expediency wait;
And ARNOLD HARRIS, in whom all the manly virtues blend,
Good soldier, clever gentleman, frank foeman, loyal friend.

One spree at Johnny Coyle's, &c.

"If these will not content you, ROBERT JOHNSON, I'll bring,
  too,
The very bravest of the brave, the truest of the true;
Implusive, generous, fearless, frank, the Senate's Paladin,
Who never did ungenerous act a victory to win.

One spree at Johnny Coyle's, &c.

"And with him JOHNNY COYLE himself, who never left a
  friend,
Nor harbored an ignoble thought, nor sought a selfish end;
The Arthur he among his knights, the pride of all his peers,
Whose soul but grows more generous, with the swift
  revolving years."

One spree at Johnny Coyle's, &c.

"Enough!" old Pluto cried; "the law must be enforced,
   'tis plain;
If with those fellows once you get, you'll ne'er return
   again;
One night would not content you, and your face would
   ne'er be seen,
After that spree at Johnny Coyle's, by me or by my Queen,

One spree at Johnny Coyle's, &c.

"And if all these fellows came at once, what would become
   of us?
They'd drown old Charon in the Styx, and murder Cer-
   berus;
Make love to all the women here, and even to my wife;
Drink all my liquor up, and be the torment of my life.

One spree at Johnny Coyle's, &c.

"They'd laugh and sing and rollick here, and turn night
   into day;
While every one his best would do to drive dull care away;
We'll take them by instalments, sir; so you may e'en
   remain,
And dismiss all hope of visiting the upper world again."

One spree at Johnny Coyle's, &c.

—198—

Now something rash would have been said by ARKANSAW, no doubt,

But the Queen winked at him, as to say, "take care what you're about!"

For very much elated was the fair Proserpine,

At the promise of unbounded fun with this good company.

One spree at Johnny Coyle's, &c.

So then she hung round Pluto's neck, and to her snowy breast

She clasped the cross old vagabond, and fondly him caressed;

And while her kisses warm and soft upon his lips did rain,

She murmured, "Let him go, my love, he'll surely come again."

One spree at Johnny Coyle's, &c.

Said he, "I won't;" said she, "Dear Lord, do let me have my way!

Let him be present at his wake! How can you say me nay?

I'm sure you do not love me; if you did, you'd not refuse,

When I want to get the fashions, and you want to hear the news."

One spree at Johnny Coyle's, &c.

And so at last the Queen prevailed, as women always do,
And thus it comes that once again this gentleman's with
you;
He's under promise to return, but that he means to break,
And many another spree to have, besides this present wake.

One spree at Johnny Coyle's, one spree at
Johnny Coyle's;
And who would not be glad to join a spree at
Johnny Coyle's?

AFTER-DINNER.

EXPLANATION.

In the winter of 1859-1860, BEVERLY TUCKER, then Counsul at Liverpool, sent JOHN F. COYLE, of Washington, a saddle of mutton, and sundry pheasants and other game. Upon this JOHN made up a dinner party of twenty, doing so on the condition that I should write *something* to be sung at table. The result was the following "werses," which were sung by JACK SAVAGE. In each verse after the sixth, a blank was left, where the person named in it was to write his name; which each did when the verse had been sung. A copy of it was transmitted to "BEV." by next mail. He had it lithographed, and sent over a few copies, of one whereof the following is a printed copy.

Of the twenty persons, eight only are now living. Worthless as a poem, the lines are priceless to me for the signatures and the memories they invoke.—[ALBERT PIKE.

Heu! Quanto minus est cum reliquis versari,
Quam istorum qui deciderunt meminisse.

AFTER DINNER.

To Beverley Tucker, Esquire, Greeting:

Dear Bev. this greeting goes to you across the Atlantic brine,
From the little room at Johnny Coyle's where once we
used to dine,
And where we've met today, to eat your mutton and your
game,
Which lately over that same brine, a welcome present came.

Of course the Host himself presides, this memorable night,
With "Jon" Kingman on his left, Will Hunter on his right;
At the foot our genial Mayor, better known as Jim Berrett,
On either hand of whom Clem Hill, and Walter Lenox sit.

Between these jovial chiefs, your friends around the table
throng;
Hugh Caperton, of martial fame, Jack Savage, full of song,
Arnold Harris, Charley Boteler, who was never known to tire,
Buck Bayliss, Robert Johnson, Charley Winder, Jim Mc-
Guire.

Knox Walker, from Tennessee, by Jonah Hoover sits,
And Albert Pike, of Arkansaw the glass ne'er pretermits:
Ned Tidball, Major Donoho, and Royal Robert Ould,
Just twenty, Bev.! you recollect the room will no more hold.

In Oeil de Perdrix, St. Marceaux, Veuve Chiquot, St. Peray,
In Liebfraunmilch, Latour, Lafitte, and ruddy Romance,
In ripe Amontillado we remember you, old friend!
And Sercial and Buel to the feast enchantment lend.

Now while old songs are carolled, and all hearts are full of
   glee,
'Tis moved and seconded, and all without demur agree,
That each shall send you greeting, in these free and easy
   rhymes,
That, redolent of fun, shall stir the memories of old times.

'Tis ordered that the host himself the first wish shall express,
And I drain the brimming bumper, to your health, and
   happiness;
Contented, prosperous, fortunate, unvexed by care or toil.
May your days glide gracefully away is the wish of JOHN
   COYLE.

May heaven its richest blessings shed upon your house and
   you,
Your enemies prove impotent, your friends prove staunch
   and true,
May your Life's current smoothly flow, nor vainly chafe and
   fret,
Against the impediments of fate! this drinks JAMES G.
   BERRET.

May all your paths be pleasantness, your life be free from
care,

Your Evening like your Morning and Meridian be fair,

And when Life's Sunset calmly comes, may all your Sky be
clear,

I, W. HUNTER, breathe this wish, heartfelt, and most sincere.

I like the good old fashioned Toast, Health, Peace and Com-
petence!

Health, on good terms, with social cheer, and foe of absti-
nence;

Peace without dulness; Competence without frugality,

All this in loving kindness BEV., E. KINGMAN wishes thee.

May heaven preserve you from all ills, this mortal state that
vex,

From all annoyances that sting, all troubles that perplex!

May no great sorrow sadden you, and no bereavement chill,

The generous heart we love so well! Thus wishes CLEMENT
HILL.

May Canvas-backs and terrapins still be within your means!

May Pheasants not destroy your taste for homely jowl and
greens!

Nor English rolls, corn-bread displace, nor any royal fish,

Make you contemn Potomac shad! I, ARNOLD HARRIS, wish.

May time take from you none you love, nor any friend
  estrange,
Nor kindliness and confidence to cold indifference change!
Nor doubt, or dumb suspicion of an old friend's truth spring
  up!
To this C. W. BOTELER drains an overflowing cup.

Let others wish you what they please, this wish, dear BEV.,
  is mine;
Soon may your chimney corner be once more your only
  shrine!
At home with loving hearts around, no longer an estray,
May you find happiness indeed! I, E. M. TIDBALL, pray.

When e'er you want to borrow, may you find a loyal friend,
Who, fortunately flush himself, will be rejoiced to lend!
You'll never want the ready will, a friend in need to aid,
And may you never want the means, J. KNOX WALKER'S wish
  is said.

May these familiar signatures, these unpretending rhymes,
Sweet memories awaken, and bring back the good old times!
Oh Barnum! may you soon return, our merriment to share!
Vouchsafe this favour, Oh ye Gods! is CHARLES H. WINDER'S
  prayer.

If Fortune will be less than kind, may she not cruel be,
Nor in her wrath afflict you with the last calamity.
May you Congressional slavery 'scape, whatever else betides:
This ROBERT W. JOHNSON asks, and asks no boon besides.

May you full long with appetite and palate unimpaired,
To feast on fish and flesh and fowl be mercifully spared!
Without that penalty the gout, which some for pleasure pay,
May you that luxury enjoy! I, BUCKNER BAYLY, pray.

Health, Wealth and Happiness! may you this three-fold boon
    attain!
May Envy, Hate and Malice, seek to injure you in vain!
And if, dear BEV., between us, Power again is put to choose,
May you the wished for office win, and J. D. HOOVER lose!

May you ne'er lose your taste for Wine, nor then potations
    choose
Nor off your feet or foundered, BEV., to drain your glass
    refuse,
Long may the generous lifeblood of the grape your wit
    inspire,
And drive away dull care, old friend! wishes JAMES C.
    MCGUIRE.

Whenever you're reported dead, and many a manly eye
With tears attest the soul's sharp pain, may it be proved a lie!
May such a wake be given *you*, as once was given *me*,
And may I, ALBERT PIKE, and all these friends be there to
  see!

When e'er again a President you help to nominate,
May *your* share of the pickings be at least a consulate!
Due meed for loyal services, may none from you withhold
Nor those you help ungrateful prove! thus wishes ROBERT
  OULD.

Should sorrows sadden you, my friend, or fortune prove
  unkind,
Receive the buffets dealt by fate, with firm and equal mind!
From whatsoever quarters ill-luck's cross-winds wildly blow,
May you as safe at anchor ride, as THOMAS DONOHO.

Dear BEV., I., JOHANN SAVAGE, drink with all my soul to this,
May all the arrows of hard fate your portly person miss!
Lord love you, BEV., and bless you with those blessings
  manifold,
Which round the home-hearth clustering, are more than
  place or gold.

May those dear ones at home be spared to make with their
    sweet eyes,

That home when to it you return, once more a Paradise!

May you with them to cherish you, long walk Life's pleasant
    ways,

And fall asleep in peace at last! Thus WALTER LENOX prays.

The last wish is assigned to me; and as when old friends part,

Hand lingers clasping hand, and heart seems clinging unto
    heart;

So I, HUGH CAPERTON, so *all* with one accord do cry,

While the voice falters at the word, *Dear* BEV., *old friend,*
    Good bye.

AULD LANG SYNE.

"Should auld acquentance be forgot,
  "And never brought to min'?
"Should auld acquentance be forgot,
  "And Auld Lang Syne?

        "For Auld Lang Syne, my Jo!
        "For Auld Lang Syne;
        "We'll tak' a cup o' kindness yet
        "For Auld Lang Syne."

"An' surely ye'll your glasses fill,
  "An' surely I'll fill mine,
"An' we'll tak' a right gude willy-wought
  "For Auld Lang Syne.
        "For Auld Lang Syne, etc.

———

'Tis mony a year sin' first we met,
  Wi' song an' jest an' wine,
And aft we saw the day-star rise
  In Auld Lang Syne,
        For Auld Lang Syne, etc.

We a' hae had our ups an' doons,
　　Great sorrows, joys divine;
And some hae won, and some hae lost,
　　Sin' Auld Lang Syne.
　　　　For Auld Lang Syne, etc.

And some hae foemen been, and charged
　　In column and in line,
Each fighting for his flag and faith,
　　And Auld Lang Syne.
　　　　For Auld Lang Syne, etc.

And they who lost, nae malice bear,
　　Nor murmur nor repine;
And they who won, the losers luve,
　　For Auld Lang Syne.
　　　　For Auld Lang Syne, etc.

And some hae seen the simmer sun
　　On mony a broad land shine,
And wandered mony a weary foot,
　　Sin' Auld Lang Syne.
　　　　For Auld Lang Syne, etc.

The laurel and the cypress on
　　Some grassy graves entwine,
Where those are laid who lo'ed us weel
　　In Auld Lang Syne.
　　　　For Auld Lang Syne, etc.

And some we luve, in foreign lands
   To see their ain land pine,
And backward look, wi' fond regret,
   To Auld Lang Syne.
       For Auld Lang Syne, etc.

We a' hae had our luves and hates—
   The hates we a' resign,
But keep the luves a' fresh and green,
   For Auld Lang Syne.
       For Auld Lang Syne, etc.

"An' there's a han', each trusty frien',
   And gi'e's a han' o' thine!
"An' we'll tak' a right gude willy-wought,
   "For Auld Lang Syne.
       "For Auld Lang Syne, etc."

An' when we shut the book o' life,
   An' a' of earth resign,
The memories shall, if sad, be sweet,
   Of Auld Lang Syne.
       For Auld Lang Syne, etc.

1869.

CRUISKEEN LAN.

Let the Statesmen swarm like bees,
At Receptions and Levees,
      And Diplomats the drawing-room adorn;
Let Patriots grow gray,
Fretting, fuming life away—
      I'm contented with my Cruiskeen Lan.

      Gra ma cree ma Cruiskeen,
      Slanthe gal ma Vourneen,
           Gra ma cree ma Cruiskeen Lan
      Gra ma cree ma Cruiskeen,
      Slanthe gal ma Vourneen,
           Gra ma cree ma Colleen ban, ban, ban,
           Gra ma cree ma Colleen ban.

Let the Great love pomp and show,
And Life's pleasures all forego,
      For Fame, that like a vapor soon is gone;
And sour old Cent-per-cent
Count his profits and his rents,—
      I am richer with my Cruiskeen Lan.

      Chorus.

Let him who great would be
Crook the hinges of the knee,
      And on Senators and Secretaries fawn;
I can not duck and bend,
But I'll always serve a friend,
      And enjoy my little Cruiskeen Lan.

Chorus.

Let him who fain would thrive,
Usurious bargains drive,
      And what he calls his soul, to Satan pawn,
I'll freely give and lend,
And the rest as freely spend,
      And enjoy my darling Cruiskeen Lan.

Chorus.

Let the Fop exhale in sighs,
At the blaze of Beauty's eyes,
      While her jewels reconcile him to her scorn;
The melted rubies shine
For us in generous wine,
      And diamonds in our Cruiskeen Lan.

Chorus.

Let Plutus have his rout,
Where you're squeezed and knocked about,
     And enjoy yourself immensely—in a horn;
Let the youthful and the gay
Enjoy the bal masque;
     Give me a quiet Cruiskeen Lan.

Chorus.

Let the banker give his feeds,
Where the modest no man heeds,
     And Parvenus on pompous Dullness fawn;
Give me a jollier set,
Of clever fellows met,
     At a friend's to taste his Cruiskeen Lan.

Chorus.

For no contracts we've to give,
Nor any posts by which to live,
     And politics we gayly laugh to scorn;
While like brothers here we stand,
Heart to heart, and hand in hand,
     With our smiling little Cruiskeen Lan.

Chorus.

More dear than gold to me
Shall the recollection be
    Of the glorious Attic nights that are gone,
When soul communed with soul,
As away the swift hours stole,
    While we drank our smiling Cruiskeen Lan.

        Chorus.

You may roam the world around
To old ocean's farthest bound;
    Visit every land the sun looks down upon;
And fellows to compare
With our set you'll find nowhere,
    When they meet to taste their Cruiskeen Lan.

        Chorus.

At JOHNNY COYLE'S, egad!
Many a frolic we have had;
    At HOOVER'S, WALLACH'S, BERRY'S seen the dawn;
At CHARLEY BOTELER'S, too,
You with me, and I with you,
    Have enjoyed our smiling Cruiskeen Lan.

        Chorus.

This evening with McGUIRE,
Fun and frolic shall conspire
     To dissipate the cares of daylight born;
And may we ne'er forget
That we here tonight were met,
     To take a kindly Cruiskeen Lan.

Chorus.

Be friend to friend more dear;
Let estrangements disappear
     As the mists that flit away before the morn;
Good-bye to jars and feud,
Let the old ties be renewed,
     As once more we take our Cruiskeen Lan.

Chorus.

1859.

"OH, JAMIE BREWED A BOWL O' PUNCH."

A SONG.

Oh, Jamie brewed a bowl of punch,
  And a' his friends to help cam' in;
A jollier set of chiels than they
  Thegither 'll ne'er be seen again.
They were na fu', they were na fu'
  But just a wee drap in their e'e;
The cock might craw and the day might daw',
  But where the punch was, aye they'd be.

Now brew the punch, McGUIRE, said he,
  And mak' it strang and make it guid,
For naething i' the warld's like punch
  To warm the heart or stir the bluid.
For we're na fu', we are na fu',
  But just a drappie in our e'e;
The cock may craw, the day may daw',
  But where the punch is, aye we'll be.

So CHARLEY BOTELER brought the bowl—
   A huge big bowl, a mighty ane,
Wherein if ony man should fa'
   He'd droon, if not himsel', his pain;
For Charley, too, he was na fu',
   But just a drappie in his e'e;
The cock might craw, the day might daw',
   But where the punch was, aye'd be he.

And neist cam' JONAH HOOVER in,
   And brought the lemons for his share,
And said "We'll ha'e a time tonight,
   "Gin I never drink a jorum mair','
For I'm na fu', I'm na that fu'
   But just a drappie in my e'e;
The cock may craw, the day may daw',
   But where the punch is, aye I'll be.

GEORGE GIDEON wi' the sugar cam',
   And dinged it i' the mighty bowl,
And cried "Mak' haste, boys, wi' your brew!"—
   For George ye see 's a thirsty soul:
He was na fu', was na that fu',
   But just a drappie in his e'e;
The cock might craw, the day might daw',
   But where the punch was, aye'd be he."

And ARNOLD HARRIS brought the tea,
  Sma' was the use he had for that,
Sin' when its taste and water's, too,
  He i' th' AULD SEVENTH had clean forgat.
He was na fu', was na that fu',
  But just a drappie in his e'e;
The cock might craw, the day might daw',
  But where the punch was, aye'd be he.

Then fu' of quips and jokes, and jests,
  Cam' waubling in douce JOHNNY COYLE
Wi' ane big jug of Farintosh,
  Auld as himself, and smooth as oil,
He was na fu', etc.

GEORGE FRENCH popped in the lumps of ice,
  Nae sign was that his heart was cauld,
And aye he trilled a merry sang,
  And syne a funny story tauld.
He was na fu', etc.

At last McGUIRE lugs out a wheen
  Great bottles filled wi' generous wine,
Whilk wi' the lave the brew completes,
  A nectar glorious and divine.

They were na fu' they were na fu',
    But just a drappie in their e'e,
The cock might craw, the day might daw',
    But where the punch was, aye they'd be.

So now the brew's a' mixed and made,
    We'll gather round it stoup in hand,
And a blither set ye shall na find
    In Pagan or in Christian land.
For we're na fu', we're na that fu',
    But just a drappie in our e'e;
The cock may craw, the day may daw',
    But where the punch is, aye we'll be.

So here's to me, and here's to you,
    To present and to absent friends,
And here's to him who patient takes
    The ills misfortune to him sends.
For we're na fu', etc.

Time taks our friends aff fast eneugh,
    And while we live we'll part wi' nane;
Aft as they err, we'll still forgi'e
    Their errors, mindfu' o' our ain.
For we're na fu', etc.

Wha first shall fail to drain his cup,
　　Nae true man shall henceforth be ca'ed;
Wha last shall fill his goblet up,
　　And drink it, shall be Prince and Lord.
For we're na fu, we are na fu',
　　But just a drappie in our e'e;
The cock may craw, the day may daw',
　　But where the punch is, aye we'll be.

　　　　　　　　　　　　1860.

"THE FINE ARKANSAS GENTLEMAN."

This was written in the winter of 1852-3, at Washington.

The credit of originating it is due to WILLIAM M. BURWELL, then of Liberty, Virginia, now of New Orleans, who was that winter at Washington,—a person of infinite humor, a capital scholar and most original thinker. He composed three or four of the verses and handed them to ALBERT PIKE, who completed the song.

The subject of it, "The Fine Arkansas Gentleman," was Major ELIAS RECTOR, of Arkansas, long a resident of that State and living near the border, or the Choctaw and Cherokee lines, but who was that winter at Washington, seeking the position of Marshal of the Arkansas district, which he had before held for several years, but lost upon the accession of President TAYLOR.

Major RECTOR was a zealous Democrat, but with many warm friends on the other side. These friendships, which were lasting ones, he owed to his genial nature, his generosity, courage, high sense of honor, and abundant hospitality. He was a person of fine presence, of great intelligence, and of an excellent and most original quaint wit; one of his peculiarities being that he wore his hair long, and put up with a comb, like a woman's. In the earlier days of Arkansas, when the strife of politics was exceedingly bitter, he was a bold, daring partizan, often engaged in personal difficulties and making many enmities, all of which he outlived. No man had a kinder heart, warmer affections, or a more true, generous and loyal nature. Nor was any man more courtly and like an English gentleman in his manners.

The song was sung for the first time when he was present, and at a party given by ROBERT W. JOHNSON, then a member of the House of Representatives, and afterwards Senator from Arkansas.

Dr. WM. P. REYBURN was a physician residing in New Orleans, and at that time in Washington. He had, many years before, lived in Arkansas, and was an intimate friend of Major RECTOR. The Doctor was immensely corpulent, and brimful of joke, jest and anecdote, a gourmand, easy and indolent, but of vigorous intellect and great shrewdness, jovial, generous, and loyally trustworthy, a better Falstaff, in all the huge Knight's good qualities, including his wit, than Hackett himself. Dear old fellow! he returned to Arkansas in 1861, a Surgeon in the Confederate Army, after an absence of more than twenty years, to die and be buried there.

PRINDLE, though the keeper of a gaming house on Pennsylvania Avenue, was a good, true, honest, generous man, whose kindness of heart and lavish bounties and his own improvidence at last made him poor. He had often returned to young men the money they had lost to his Bank; and was therefore liked and respected by many who knew him well, and among whom many had National reputation.— [Note by Gen. PIKE.

I.

Now all good fellows, listen, and a story I will tell
Of a mighty clever gentleman who lives extremely well
In the western part of Arkansas, close to the Indian line,
Where he gets drunk once a week on whisky, and immediately
    sobers himself completely on the very best of wine;
        A fine Arkansas gentleman,
        Close to the Choctaw line!

II.

This fine Arkansas gentleman has a mighty fine estate
Of five or six thousand acres or more of land, that will be
    worth a great deal some day or other if he don't kill
    himself too soon, and will only condescend to wait;
And four or five dozen negroes that would rather work than
    not,
And such quantities of horses, and cattle, and pigs, and other
    poultry, that he never pretends to know how many he
    has got;
        This fine Arkansas gentleman,
        Close to the Choctaw line!

III.

This fine Arkansas gentleman has built a splendid house

On the edge of a big prairie, extremely well populated with
deer, and hares, and grouse;

And when he wants to feast his friends he has nothing more
to do

Than to leave the pot-lid off, and the decently behaved birds
fly straight into the pot, knowing he'll shoot them if they
don't; and he has a splendid stew,

> This fine Arkansas gentleman,
>
> Close to the Choctaw line!

IV.

This fine Arkansas gentleman makes several hundred bales,

Unless from drought or worm, a bad stand, or some other
damned contingency, his crop is short or fails;

And when its picked, and ginned, and baled, he puts it on
a boat,

And gets aboard himself likewise, and charters the bar, and
has a devil of a spree, while down to New Orleans he
and his cotton float,

> This fine Arkansas gentleman,
>
> Close to the Choctaw line!

V.

And when he gets to New Orleans he sacks a clothing store,

And puts up at the City Hotel, the St. Louis, the St. Charles, the Veranda, and all the other hotels in the city, if he succeeds in finding any more;

Then he draws upon his merchant, and goes about and treats,

Every man from Kentucky, and Arkansas, and Alabama, and Virginia, and the Choctaw nation, and every other damned vagabond he meets!

> This fine Arkansas gentleman,
>
> Close to the Choctaw line!

VI.

The last time he was down there, when he thought of going back,

After staying about fifteen days, more or less, he discovered that by lending and by spending, and being a prey in general to gamblers, hackmen, loafers, brokers, hoosiers, tailors, servants, and many other individuals, white and black,

He distributed his assets, and got rid of all his means,

And had nothing left to show for them, barring two or three headaches, an invincible thirst, and an extremely general and promiscuous acquaintance in the aforesaid New Orleans;

> This fine Arkansas gentleman,
>
> Close to the Choctaw line!

VII.

Now how this gentleman got home is neither here nor there,

But I've been credibly informed that he swore worse than forty-seven pirates, and fiercely combed his hair;

And after he got safely home, they say he took an oath

That he'd never bet a cent again at any game of cards, and moreover, for want of decent advisers, he foreswore whiskey and women both;

This fine Arkansas gentleman,

Close to the Choctaw line!

VIII.

This fine Arkansas gentleman went strong for Pierce and King,

And so came on to Washington to get a nice fat office, or some other equally comfortable thing;

But like him from Jerusalem that went to Jericho,

He fell among thieves again, and could not win a bet whether he coppered it or not, so his cash was bound to go—

This fine Arkansas gentleman,

Close to the Choctaw line!

IX.

So when his moneys all were gone, he took unto his bed,

And Dr. Reyburn physicked him, and the chamber-maid, who had a great affection for him, with her arm held up his head;

And all his friends came weeping round, and bidding him adieu.

And two or three dozen preachers, whom he didn't know at all, and didn't care a damn if he didn't, came praying for him too;

> This fine Arkansas gentleman,
>
> Close to the Choctaw line!

X.

They closed his eyes and laid him out all ready for the tomb,

And merely to console themselves they opened the biggest kind of game of faro right there in his own room;

But when he heard the checks, he flung the linen off his face, and sung out just precisely as he used to do when he was alive, "Prindle, don't turn! hold on! I go twenty on the king, and copper on the ace!"

> This fine Arkansas gentleman,
>
> Close to the Choctaw line!

AN AUNCIENTE FYTTE

Pleasaunte and full of Pastyme of

A DOLLAR, OR TWO.

With circumspect steps as we pick our way through
This intricate world, as all prudent folks do,
May we still on our journey be able to view
The benevolent face of a Dollar, or two.
    For an excellent thing is a Dollar, or two;
    No friend is so staunch as a Dollar, or two;
        In country or town,
        As we stroll up and down,
We are cock of the walk, with a Dollar, or two.

Do you wish to emerge from the bachelor-crew,
And a charming young innocent female to woo?
You must always be ready the handsome to do,
Although it may cost you a Dollar, or two.
    For love tips his darts with a Dollar, or two;
    Young affections are gained by a Dollar, or two;
        And beyond all dispute,
        The best card of your suit
Is the eloquent chink of a Dollar, or two.

Do you wish to have friends who your bidding will do,
And help you your means to get speedily through?
You'll find them remarkably faithful and true,
By the magical power of a Dollar, or two.
  For friendship's secured by a Dollar, or two;
  Popularity's gained by a Dollar, or two;
        And you'll ne'er want a friend
        Till you no more can lend,
And yourself need to borrow a Dollar, or two.

Do you wish in the Courts of the Country to sue
For the right or estate that's another man's due?
Your lawyer will surely remember his cue,
When his palm you have crossed with a Dollar, or two.
  For a lawyer's convinced with a Dollar, or two,
  And a jury set right with a Dollar, or two;
        And though justice *is* blind,
        Yet a way you may find
To open her eyes with a Dollar, or two.

Do you want a snug place where there's little to do,
Or at Government cost foreign countries to view?
A contract to get, or a patent renew?
You can make it all right, with a Dollar, or two.
    For merit is proved by a Dollar, or two,
    And a patriot's known by a Dollar, or two;
            Civil service rules?—Oh, oh!
            They're all humbug, you know;
Just use with discretion a Dollar, or two.

If a claim that is proved to be honestly due,
Department or Congress you'd quickly put through,
And the chance for its payment begins to look blue,
You can help it along with a Dollar, or two.
    For votes are secured by a Dollar, or two,
    And influence bought by a Dollar, or two;
            And he'll come to grief
            Who depends for relief
Upon justice not braced with a Dollar, or two.

Do you wish that the Press should the decent thing do,
And give your reception a gushing review,
Describing the dresses by stuff, style and hue?
Hand Jenkins in private a Dollar, or two,
    For the pen sells its praise for a Dollar, or two,
    And squirts its abuse for a Dollar, or two,
        As contractors sell votes,
        And the banks discount notes,
That are not worth a damn, for a Dollar, or two.

Do you wish your existence with faith to imbue,
And so become one of the sanctified few?
To enjoy a good name and a well-cushioned pew,
You must freely come down with a Dollar, or two.
    For the Gospel is preached for a Dollar, or two,
    Salvation is reached by a Dollar, or two;
        Sins are pardoned, sometimes,
        But the worst of all crimes
Is to find yourself *short* of a Dollar, or two.

ANTHEM No. 1.

Among the dead our Brothers sleep,
    Their lives were rounded true and well;
And Love in bitter sorrow weeps
    Above their dark and silent cell.

No pain, no anxious sleepless Fear
    Invades their house; no mortal woes
Their narrow resting-place come near,
    To trouble their serene repose.

Their names are graven on the stones
    That friendship's tears will often wet;
But each true Brother's heart upon
    That name is stamped more deeply yet.

As Hiram slept, the widow's son,
    So do our Brothers take their rest;
Life's battle fought, Life's duties done,
    Their faults forgot, their worth confessed.

So let them sleep that dreamless sleep,
    Our sorrows clustering round each head;
Be comforted, ye loved, who weep!
    They live with God; they are not dead.

ANTHEM No. 2.

Mourn not them whose stars have set,
While the light is with us yet;
While remembered words are dear,
While their spirits meet us here.

Though the blast shake down the fruit,
Though the leaves drop on the root,
When the death-wind withering blows,
Still the great tree, broadening, grows,

Nothing done is done in vain,
Words and deeds alike remain;
Memories soft and sad become
Angels luring us to home.

Humblest men do mightier things
Often than the sceptered kings;
Roughest paths, by Virtue trod,
Lead the nearest way to God.

Living men are heavenward led
By the errors of the Dead;
Murmur not, but work and pray;
Death is Heaven's dawn of day.

ODE.

(SUNG AT THE CELEBRATION OF THE I. O. O. F.)

The night cometh swiftly, the thick clouds are drifting
  Around the dark mountains that rampart the plain;
The storm, its tumultuous surges uplifting,
  Is calling its hosts to the foray again.

The surf, white with foam, round the sun madly dashes,
  As waves dash against a lone ship near the shore;
The lightning at intervals gloomily flashes,
  And over the plain moans the thunder's hoarse roar.

The night comes with darkness, the night comes with terror,
  The storm with his armies rides fast by her side,—
Wo, wo, to the way-farer wand'ring in error,
  To whom the glad sight of his home is denied!

Lo! weary and way-worn comes fainting a stranger,
  Whose feet with their blood stain the pitiless ground;—
Where, where, shall we seek for a refuge from danger,
  Where hide when the storm hurls its arrows around?

Lo! feeble with terror his weak footsteps falter,
  He thinks with despair of the pleasures of home,
He seemeth a victim, the desert an altar,
  The far-flashing lightning his sentence of doom.

What is it that suddenly calms his emotions,
　　Gives strength to his feet that were ready to fail?
'Tis a tent gleams ahead, as far off on the ocean,
　　The foundering sailor descries a white sail.

Haste onward, lone brother the storm howleth o'er thee,
　　Loud roars the wild wind, fiercely beats the cold rain;—
'Tis an Odd Fellows' Camp that lies calmly before thee,
　　And none there for shelter and food ask in vain.

The Sentinel hails, his lone vigil that keepeth;
　　The stranger is welcomed, is sheltered and fed;
Without still the storm roars, but calmly he sleepeth,
　　While Love, Truth and Friendship encircle his bed.

Ho! wake thee up, Brother! the fresh day is dawning,
　　The storm that beset thee has fled far away;—
Eat, Brother, and drink! then set onward this morning!
　　Thy children shall greet thee while yet it is day.

And henceforth when humbly and tearfully kneeling,
　　Thy heart with devotion and gratitude warm,
Forget not the night when the thunder was pealing,
　　And the Odd Fellows' Camp shone a star through the storm.

ODES

sung in the

SUBLIME ORDER OF GOOD SAMARITANS.

In Part Written, in part Selected and Changed for the Order

by

GENERAL ALBERT PIKE, 33°,

Gr. Com. Sup. Council, South. Jurisd.

1877.

No. 1.

I faint, I fall; my wearied feet are bleeding;
    I starve, I thirst, am hopeless and forlorn;
No generous heart my cry for help is heeding;
    When will the long night end? when come the morn?

    The burden of sad hearts that break,
        Should rest upon our own;
    The widow's want, the orphan's cry,
        The hungry workman's moan.

    Let us all learn what this word means
        That God gave us to keep;
    "Rejoice with them that do rejoice,
        "And weep with them that weep."

No. 2.

Sow thou then, with generous hand,
    Help for want and pain;
Faint not for hot Summer's days,
    Nor for cold Spring's rain:
Wait! till ripening Autumn brings
    Sheaves of golden grain;
Bread upon the waters cast,
    Comes to us again.

No. 3.

Let not our Sister walk in vain,
    Life's pleasant shaded ways,
Not helping those who fainting toil,
    Or count the workless days:
For "Soul that gives is Soul that lives;"
    To bear another's load
Makes light one's own, makes short the way,
    Makes bright the homeward road.

No. 4.

Sweet be her dreams, the fair, the young!
Grace, beauty, breathe upon her!
Music! haunt thou about her tongue!
Life! fill her path with honor!

All golden thoughts, all wealth of days,
Truth, Friendship, Love, surround her!
So may she smile till life be closed
And angel hands have crowned her.

Dirge.—No. 5.

Go and dig my grave today!
Weary of my wanderings all,
Now from earth I pass away,
For the heavenly peace doth call;
Angel voices from above
Call me to their rest and love.

Go and dig my grave today!
Homeward doth my journey tend,
And I lay my staff away,
Here where all things earthly end;
In the only painless bed
Now I lay my aching head.

No. 6.

God speaks from Paradise, and says,
    "I gave the gift of life;
"Wert thou not called in many ways?
    "Are earth and heaven at strife?
"I gave thee of my seed to sow,
    "Hast brought my hundred-fold?"
Canst thou reply, with face a-glow,
    "Dear God! here is thy gold?"

No. 7.

Sow on! the hours are fleeting fast,
    The seed must drop today;
What though the time come not to reap,
    Before you pass away?
What though your tears rain on the seed?
    They'll stir its quiet sleep,
The green blades will more quickly rise
    For every tear you weep.

No. 8.

We hear the reapers singing, who
    Into God's harvest go;
Who at the gates of night, whom they
    Invite, will grope below?
Sow on! and thus climb surely up
    To where the light appears;
Where you shall reap in gladness what
    You sow today in tears.

———

A Song, for the I. O. O. F., by Bro. A. B. Grosh, of Pa.,
modified by Albert Pike.

"*In God we trust,*" was sweetly sung
    By every morning star on high;
"*In God* we trust," right gladly rung,
    From sons of God in loud reply;—
When from old chaos systems rolled,
    From darkness, light, in rosy youth.
And Faith wrapped in her clouds of gold,
    Awoke to *Friendship, Love* and *Truth.*

"In God we trust," the golden sun
    And silver moon yet seem to say;
And all the stars that round them burn,
    Repeat the anthem night and day;
And all our earth, from hill and vale,
    From all that live and breathe and move,
Where footsteps fall, where flows a sail,
    Responds with "Friendship, Truth and Love!"

"In God we trust," the Builders said,
    And deep in earth they sunk the wall;
In Hope the corner stone is laid,
    Now raise the proud and lofty Hall.
May no sad accident befall,
    No loss of life or loss of limb,
But may we meet here, one and all,
    To sing the dedication hymn.

Here may we, with *Fidelity*,
>Our sacred *covenant* fulfill;

Here may *Remembrance* perfect be,
>And *Truth* inspire our bosoms still.

May *Hospitality* here reign,
>With *Toleration, Trust* and *Love*;

And *Faith* each earnest soul sustain,
>Until we reach *Thy Tent* above.

"In Thee we trust," and thus to *Thee*,
>We offer all, *for all is Thine;*

That Thy good stewards we may be,
>On earth, in word and work divine.

When Brothers want, when Death lays low,
>When orphans cry in helpless youth;

When widows weep in cheerless woe,
>Fill us with *"Friendship, Love* and *Truth!"*

SONG OF THE NABAJO.

Who rideth as fleet as a fleet Nabajo?
Whose arm is so strong with the lance and the bow?
His arrow in battle as lightning is swift;
His march is the course of the mountainous drift.

The Eutaw can ride down the deer of the hills,
With his shield ornamented with bald-eagle quills;
Our houses are full of the skins he has drest;
We have slaves of his women, the brightest and best.

Go, talk of the strength of a valiant Paiute,
He will hide in the trees when our arrows we shoot;
And who knows the wild Coyotera to tame,
But the bold Nabajo, with his arrow of flame?

The Moqui may boast from his town of the Rock:
Can it stand when the earthquake shall come with its shock?
The Suni may laugh in his desert so dry—
He will wail to his God when our foray is nigh.

Oh, who is so brave as a mountain Apache?
He can come to our home when the doors we unlatch,
And plunder our women when we are away;
When met he our braves in their battle array?

Whose mouth is so big as a Spaniard's at home?
But if *we* rush along like the cataract foam,
And sweep off his cattle and herds from his stall,
Oh, then to the saints who so loudly can call?

Up, then, and away! Let the quiver be full!
And as soon as the stars make the mountain air cool,
The fire of the harvest shall make heaven pale,
And the priesthood shall curse, and the coward shall wail.

And there will be counting of beads then to do—
And the Pueblos shall mount and prepare to pursue;
But when could their steeds, so mule-footed and slow,
Compare with the birds of the free Nabajo?

1832.

WAR SONG OF THE COMANCHES.

Oh, who with the sons of the plains can compete,
When from west, south and north like the torrents they meet?
And when doth the face of the white trader blanch,
Except when at moonrise he hears the Commanche?

Will you speak in our lodge of a bold Caiawah?
He is brave, but it is when our braves are afar;
Will you talk of the gun of the Arapeho?
Go—first see the arrow spring off from our bow.

The white wolf goes with us wherever we ride;
For food there is plenty on every side;
And Mexican bones he has plenty to cranch,
When he follows the troop of the flying Comanche.

The Toyah exults in his spear and his shield,
And the Wequah—but both have we taught how to yield;
And the Panana horses our women now ride,
While their scalps in our lodges are hung side by side.

Let the Wawsashy boast; he will run like a deer,
When afar on the prairie our women appear;
The shaven scalps hang, in each lodge three or four—
We will count them again, and ere long there'll be more.

The Gromonts came down—'tis three summers ago—
To look for our scalps and to hunt buffalo;
But they turned to the mountains their faces again,
And the trace of their lodges is washed out by rain.

The spirit above never sends us his curse,
And the buffalo never gets angry with us;
We are strong as the storm! we are free as the breeze!
And we laugh at the power of the pale Ikanese.

The mountain Shoshones have hearts big and strong;
Our brothers they are, and they speak the same tongue;
And let them in battle but stand by our side,
And we scorn Ikanese and black Spaniard allied.

Oo-no-ha! Come out from the Brazos Canon!
Let us range to the head of the salt Semaron!
For our horses are swift, and there's hair to be won,
When the Ikanese wagons their track are upon.

1832.